KLAUS BRUMMER

A LEADER-CENTERED THEORY OF FOREIGN POLICY CHANGE

U.S. Foreign Policy toward Cuba under Obama

First published in Great Britain in 2024 by

Bristol University Press
University of Bristol
1–9 Old Park Hill
Bristol
BS2 8BB
UK
t: +44 (0)117 374 6645
e: bup-info@bristol.ac.uk

Details of international sales and distribution partners are available at
bristoluniversitypress.co.uk

© Bristol University Press 2024

British Library Cataloguing in Publication Data
A catalogue record for this book is available from the British Library

ISBN 978-1-5292-3770-2 hardcover
ISBN 978-1-5292-3771-9 ePub
ISBN 978-1-5292-3772-6 ePdf

The right of Klaus Brummer to be identified as author of this work has been
asserted by him in accordance with the Copyright, Designs and Patents Act 1988.

All rights reserved: no part of this publication may be reproduced, stored in
a retrieval system, or transmitted in any form or by any means, electronic,
mechanical, photocopying, recording, or otherwise without the prior permission
of Bristol University Press.

Every reasonable effort has been made to obtain permission to reproduce copyrighted
material. If, however, anyone knows of an oversight, please contact the publisher.

The statements and opinions contained within this publication are solely those
of the author and not of the University of Bristol or Bristol University Press.
The University of Bristol and Bristol University Press disclaim responsibility
for any injury to persons or property resulting from any material published
in this publication.

Bristol University Press works to counter discrimination on
grounds of gender, race, disability, age and sexuality.

Cover design: Blu Inc
Front cover image: Shutterstock / GagliardiPhotography
Bristol University Press uses environmentally responsible
print partners.
Printed and bound in Great Britain by CPI Group (UK) Ltd,
Croydon, CR0 4YY

To my little 'co-worker' Jeremy ...
　　... and the Blue Jays

Contents

List of Figures and Tables		vi
List of Abbreviations		vii
Acknowledgments		viii
one	Introduction	1
two	A Leader-Centered Theory of Foreign Policy Change	15
three	U.S. Foreign Policy Change toward Cuba under Obama	54
four	Alternative Explanations	107
five	Conclusion and Outlook	117
Appendix 1: Trump's Political Beliefs on Cuba		127
Appendix 2: Expectations for Donald Trump as Policy Entrepreneur		129
Notes		131
References		135
Index		162

List of Figures and Tables

Figures

2.1	Analytical framework	19
3.1	Comparison of the political beliefs of U.S. presidents Bush and Obama on Cuba	75
A.1	Comparison of the political beliefs of U.S. presidents Obama and Trump on Cuba	127

Tables

2.1	Philosophical and instrumental beliefs in Operational Code Analysis	29
2.2	Behavioral implications of political beliefs	32
2.3	Policy entrepreneurial actions and leadership traits	44
2.4	Source text requirements for Operational Code Analysis and Leadership Trait Analysis	50
3.1	Key events in U.S.–Cuban relations during the Obama presidency	57
3.2	Examples of major changes in U.S.–Cuba policy under the Obama administration	64
3.3	Obama's leadership traits	81
3.4	Obama's use of policy entrepreneurial instruments	83
A.1	Trump's leadership traits	130

List of Abbreviations

BACE	Belief in the ability to control events
CC	Conceptual complexity
DIS	Distrust of others
FPA	Foreign Policy Analysis
IGB	In-group bias
LTA	Leadership Trait Analysis
NSPM	National Security Presidential Memorandum
OAS	Organization of American States
OCA	Operational Code Analysis
PPD	Presidential Policy Directive
PWR	Need for power
SC	Self-confidence
TASK	Task focus
UNGA	United Nations General Assembly
VICS	Verbs in Context System

Acknowledgments

This book highlights the role of leaders in bringing about major foreign policy change. While leaders are often times associated with fundamental redirections in their countries' foreign policy, in the sense of "only Nixon could go to China," more often than not their specific influence is more assumed than really shown. This is not to say that structures or contexts do not matter. However, extant research suggests that structures in themselves do not determine foreign policy. Indeed, leaders respond differently to environmental incentives and constraints. This, in turn, should also have implications for episodes of major redirections of foreign policy. Against this background, this book presents a "leader-centered theory of foreign policy change" based on which the independent, systematic, and predictable effect of leaders on the "why" (that is, what triggers foreign policy change), the "what" (that is, the substantive direction in which a policy is changed), and the "how" (that is, what leaders do to put aspired changes into practice) of foreign policy change can be ascertained.

Draft chapters have been presented at the European Workshops in International Studies (EWIS), the annual conferences of the International Studies Association (ISA) and the British International Studies Association (BISA) respectively, and the Indiana University World Politics Research Seminar. Many thanks indeed to everyone who provided comments on those occasions, with special thanks due to Sibel Oktay, Kai Oppermann, Juliet Kaarbo, and Šumit Ganguly. Similar thanks go to the anonymous reviewers for their constructive comments and suggestions, and to the Bristol University Press team, and Stephen Wenham in particular, for their assistance and support throughout the process.

ONE

Introduction

> [T]he changes that I announced to U.S. policy toward Cuba mark the beginning of a new relationship between the people of the United States and the people of Cuba.
> President Obama, 7th Summit of the Americas, April 11, 2015[1]

What a difference a president makes. For decades, the United States' relationship with neighboring Cuba had been mired in an antagonism that dated back to the late 1950s and included the Bay of Pigs invasion, the Cuban missile crisis, and several failed attempts to murder the Cuban leader Fidel Castro, among other things (for example, Schoultz, 2009). Then, during the presidency of Barack Obama U.S.–Cuban relations experienced a fundamental shift. Often times referred to as "Cuban thaw" especially by the media (for example, BBC, 2015; Hirschfeld Davis, 2015c; Phillips, 2015; *The Economist*, 2016a), the turnaround was actually much more far-reaching than the thawing metaphor suggests. Indeed, the president "ventured into diplomatic territory where the last 10 presidents refused to go" (Baker, 2014), culminating in the reestablishment of diplomatic relations after more than 50 years and the first visit to Cuba of a sitting U.S. president in Cuba in more than 85 years. One commentator even opined that those actions "finally ended the Cold War" (DeYoung, 2016). The question that this book seeks to explore concerns the role that President Obama played in this fundamental reorientation of U.S.–Cuba policy.

To some, this question might seem striking, if not outright puzzling. After all, why would policy changes ushered in by the Obama administration not be tied to the president? Indeed, episodes of major reorientations of countries' foreign policies are often times associated with the leaders during whose tenure those changes occurred, including Richard Nixon in terms of U.S. foreign policy toward China, Willy Brandt for Western German policy toward the Soviet Bloc, or Yitzhak Rabin for Israeli policy toward the Palestinians. However, Foreign Policy Analysis (FPA) scholarship, which refers to theory-driven explanations of foreign policy processes and outcomes (for example, Brummer and Oppermann, 2024; Kaarbo and Thies, 2024), is surprisingly indeterminate when it comes to accounting for the specific and distinct role of individual leaders in bringing about major redirections of foreign policy.

The goal of this book is to contribute to the theoretical discussion by proposing a "leader-centered theory of foreign policy change" that places individual leaders front and center in the explanation of episodes of major redirections in a country's foreign policy. In addition, it seeks to make an empirical contribution by examining the case of U.S. foreign policy change toward Cuba under the Obama administration. That case has been generally underexplored so far from the vantage point of theory-driven explanations of foreign policy change. In addition, scholarship remains diffuse in terms of the specific role that President Obama had in driving this process forward.

The remainder of this introduction proceeds in six steps. The next section reviews the FPA literature on foreign policy change and highlights the lack of clarity concerning the role of leaders as drivers, or agents, of major foreign policy change. The following section introduces core tenets of the "leader-centered theory of foreign policy change" whose aim is to address the aforementioned shortcoming. The discussion then turns to the empirical case to which the leader-centered theory is applied, in form of changes in U.S. foreign policy toward Cuba during the Obama administration. Next, alternative explanatory factors are introduced that the FPA literature proposes as key drivers of foreign policy change and which potentially may provide equally good, if not better, explanations for the case under examination. The penultimate section discusses the aspired contributions of this book to the scholarly debate about foreign policy change in general and the specific case of U.S. foreign policy change toward Cuba in particular. The introduction concludes with a brief plan of the book.

FPA scholarship on foreign policy change

The FPA literature points to multiple drivers of foreign policy change which are located on all of the three "images" proposed by Kenneth Waltz (1959), hence the level of international system, the domestic level, and the level of individual leaders respectively. Typically, the identified independent and/or intervening factors (or variables) from different levels of analysis are interwoven in rather complex models that seek to account for foreign policy change (for example, Goldmann, 1982; Holsti, 1982; Hermann, 1990; Carlsnaes, 1993; Rosati, 1994; Gustavsson, 1999; Kleistra and Mayer, 2001; Welch, 2005; Hermann, 2012; Blavoukos and Bourantonis, 2014; Joly and Haesebrouck, 2021). Crucially for the purpose of this book, virtually all models of foreign policy change ascribe some importance to individual leaders in bringing about that outcome.

For example, Charles Hermann lists individual leaders as one of four "primary change agents" (next to bureaucratic advocacy, domestic restructuring, and external shocks) and argues that foreign policy change could "result[] from the determined efforts of an authoritative policy-maker, frequently the head of government, who imposes his own vision of the basic redirection necessary in foreign policy" (Hermann, 1990: 11). In turn, Kalevi Holsti, whose model of foreign policy change contains three independent variables (external factors, domestic factors, and background historical and cultural factors), suggests that those variables are filtered through several, mostly leader-related intervening variables in order to produce foreign policy restructuring. Indeed, it is the perceptions/calculations of decision makers, their personality factors, and elite attitudes toward external actors together with the policy-making process that serve as prisms through which the independent variables are construed or as filters through which they have to pass (Holsti, 1982: 12–15).

In turn, Jakob Gustavsson (1999: 86) ascribes agency to individual decision makers since their cognition/perception of the international and domestic factors is considered as crucial for ushering in foreign policy changes as is their role as "policy entrepreneur[s] who capitalize[] on a shift in the political conditions and manage[] to launch a favourite political proposal." In his "loss-aversion theory of foreign policy change," David Welch weaves together organizational processes, the role of leaders' motives and cognition pertaining to imminent or actual policy failure (that is, "painful costs"), and leaders' risk propensity (Welch, 2005: Chapter 2). Last but not least, in their discussion of possible "carriers" or, for that matter, "barriers" of foreign policy change, Yvonne Kleistra and Igor Mayer (2001) emphasize the role of leaders next to factors located at the level of the international system, the national political system, and organizational level.

Overall, then, the literature on the drivers of foreign policy change suggests that leaders can be highly relevant for foreign policy change. At the same time, the preceding discussion has shown that leader-specific variables usually tend to be incorporated into multi-causal models. As a result, those models render it all but impossible to ascertain any *independent and systematic* effect of the idiosyncratic features and characteristics of leaders on foreign policy change. What is more, while acknowledging the importance of leaders in general terms, for instance with respect to cognition, perception, or risk propensity, the models tend to be rather vague as to what exactly it is about leaders' cognition, perception, and so on that is of consequence for explaining foreign policy change. By extension, the models offer little insight into how those characteristics can be empirically ascertained, thus "measured," in the first place.

For instance, while Welch (2005) uses prospect theory to ascertain leaders' risk propensity, this is just one of three variables (next to ones based on organizational theory and cognitive/motivational psychology) that account for foreign policy change in his model. Similarly, while Hermann (1990) points to the importance of leaders' cognition (for example, perception of external shocks or recognition of policy discrepancies), he does not explore in any greater detail how, for instance, leader-specific psychological or cognitive dispositions influence such perceptions or recognitions, let alone how they can be identified. A similar picture emerges from Gustavsson's work. While he too emphasizes the importance of "change in [leaders'] beliefs" (1999: 84) as a precondition for foreign policy change to occur, he does not explicate the structure of those beliefs, nor how they, and changes therein, can be measured.

In short, on the one hand, existing explanatory frameworks of foreign policy change do assign a certain role to leaders. On the other hand, the typically multi-causal frameworks, which integrate structural and actor-specific variables, make it next to impossible to identify any independent effects of leaders on foreign policy change. In addition, they also tend to be rather vague regarding what exactly it is about leaders that matters in this context as well as how to empirically ascertain those relevant characteristics in the first place (Brummer and Oppermann, 2021: 325–6).

The "leader-centered theory of foreign policy change" proposed in this volume seeks to address those shortcomings. It builds on and extends the few works on foreign policy change that explicitly evolve around leaders. Most notably, Yi Edward Yang (2010) and Guy Ziv (2011) emphasize respectively the importance of leaders' conceptual complexity (in the case of the United States) and cognitive structure (in the case of Israel) as drivers of foreign policy change. Thus, these authors do emphasize the role of leaders' traits and cognitive abilities. What they refrain from doing, however, is to embed leaders into broader political dynamics, which is what the proposed leader-centered theory tries to accomplish as well.

Therefore, although this book places individual decision makers front and center in its explanation of foreign policy change, this is not to suggest that structural factors are irrelevant. Indeed, such factors do shape the political environment within which leaders have to operate. However, structural factors do not automatically translate into foreign policy decisions. Rather, it is the apperception of the structural factors, thus the political environment, by leaders through which those factors become meaningful. This has been emphasized not only by several of the aforementioned models of foreign policy change but also already by Harold and Margaret Sprout in their classic discussion of the effect of environmental factors on leaders' decision-making (Sprout and Sprout, 1957). Yet is it not only that the perception of the environment by decision makers matters. As importantly, decades' worth of work on leadership profiling in FPA have shown that leaders can and often times do perceive one and the same context very differently and, as importantly, resulting from certain personal characteristics and differences therein from leader to leader, respond to and act in those perceived environments in very different ways (for example, Post, 2005).

Against this background, this book takes as its points of departure that (a) structural factors, both international and domestic ones, are underdetermined, thus not sufficient to explain foreign policy change; and that (b) leaders have an independent effect on the initiation, direction, and implementation of foreign policy change. In other words, the influence of leaders on foreign policy change extends beyond what can already be explained by structural factors. It is against this background that this book proposes a "leader-centered theory of foreign policy change" which can be used to identify and trace the independent, systematic, and predictable influence and effect of individual leaders in bringing about major adjustments of a country's foreign policy.

A leader-centered theory of foreign policy change

The 'leader-centered theory of foreign policy change' highlights the role of individual decision makers as drivers of foreign policy change. Contrary to most of the works discussed in the previous section, it does not integrate leadership variables into a broader framework that renders it to next to impossible to discern any specific role of leaders. Rather, it seeks to ascertain the independent, systematic, and predictable effect that individual leaders may have on the substance and process of major foreign policy change. From this perspective, it is imperative to identify idiosyncratic characteristics of leaders. To that end, the proposed theory draws on two well-established analytical constructs from FPA, in form of Operational Code Analysis (OCA) and Leadership Trait Analysis (LTA), based on which leaders' political beliefs and leadership traits respectively can be identified. Specific manifestations of those characteristics can be connected to different phases of foreign policy redirection, as will be highlighted in greater detail later in the book.

Another major difference to existing approaches to explain foreign policy change is that the leader-centered theory of foreign policy change systematically incorporates insights from public policy scholarship. True, in recent years that has been an increased interest in applying analytical frameworks that have been originally developed to explain public policy making and outcomes to the realm of foreign policy (for a general discussion on the promises and pitfalls of bringing together FPA and public policy scholarship, see Lentner, 2006; Charillon, 2018; Kaarbo, 2019b). Works along those lines have demonstrated that public policy theories can be successfully applied for that purpose (for example, Brummer et al, 2019). However, what has been largely missing in the discussion are more targeted efforts that aim at actual cross-fertilization between the two literatures by bringing together insights from the respective fields into one explanatory framework. As I have recently argued elsewhere (Brummer, 2024), a promising starting point to that effect is to focus on specific substantive issue areas that are of interest to both literatures and explore how bringing together insights from the respective field contributes to getting a firmer analytical and empirical handle of the empirical phenomenon under examination. Thus, this book incorporates insights from two distinct strands of public policy scholarship, on policy failures on the one hand and on policy entrepreneurs on the other, in its effort to develop a novel theory for grasping foreign policy change.

More specifically, the leader-centered theory of foreign policy change, whose goal is to explore major changes in a country's foreign policy, seeks to provide answers to the "why," the "what," and the "how" of foreign policy change:

- The "why" concerns the reasons that make leaders seek to redirect existing foreign policy. The theory refers to this as "triggering change" and suggests that a leader's diagnosis of a failing or failed policy is the key trigger for pursuing policy change. The discussion is grounded in the public policy scholarship on policy failures.
- The "what" relates to the substantive direction in which foreign policy change should unfold from the perspective of a leader. The theory refers to this as "guiding change" and proposes that leaders' political beliefs provide guidance in this regard. The discussion is based in FPA scholarship and OCA in particular.
- The "how" is in reference to what leaders who act as policy entrepreneurs do in order to bring about foreign policy change in the domestic political arena. The theory refers to this as "implementing change" and proposes that leaders'

choice of policy entrepreneurial instruments is a function of their leadership traits. The discussion combines insights from public policy scholarship on policy entrepreneurs and FPA scholarship in the form of LTA.

The goal of the leader-centered theory is to account for major changes in a country's foreign policy.

Such changes are not confined to a single decision but entail far-reaching policy adjustments across multiple domains of action (Hermann, 1990). They cover both fundamental changes in rhetoric (words) and actions (deeds). Chapter Two of this volume presents the different elements of the leader-centered theory of foreign policy change in greater detail.

The empirical case: U.S. foreign policy toward Cuba under the Obama administration

In order to explore the plausibility of the proposed leader-centered theory of foreign policy, the latter is applied in Chapter Three of this volume to the case of U.S. policy toward Cuba during the Obama administration. On the one hand, there is no shortage in general discussions of U.S. foreign policy toward Cuba and of U.S.–Cuban relations (for example, Schoultz, 2009; Gibbs, 2011; Castro Mariño and Pruessen, 2012; LeoGrande and Kornbluh, 2014). Two issues have been examined in particular. One is the trade embargo (for example, Giuliano, 1998; Kaplowitz, 1998; Schwab, 1999; Haney and Vanderbush 2005; LeoGrande, 2015a; White, 2015). The other is the influence of the Cuban lobby in the United States on American foreign policy toward Cuba (for example, Haney and Vanderbush, 1999; Rubenzer, 2008; Pérez, 2014; LeoGrande, 2020). Some studies have also connected those two issue areas (for example, Rubenzer and Redd, 2010; Rubenzer, 2011; Haney, 2018).

On the other hand, the specific episode that this book focuses on, in form of the Cuba policy of the Obama administration, has received limited attention thus far. This is surprising not only in that it offers a major departure from extent U.S. policy in an issue area that has been examined quite extensively as such, as shown, but also because it represents one of the key foreign policy hallmarks of the Obama administration. Among the works that have covered Obama's Cuba policy, most approach the topic from a historical or policy-oriented perspective (for example, Prevost, 2011; LeoGrande and Jiménez, 2012: 368–71; LeoGrande and Kornbluh, 2014: Chapter 9; Pérez, 2014: 155–7; Hoffmann, 2015; LeoGrande, 2015a; Crahan and Castro Mariño, 2016; Haney, 2018: 175–7; Rodriguez and Targ, 2018: 599–602; Kornbluh and LeoGrande, 2019; Laguardia Martinez et al, 2020: Chapters 5–7). This includes accounts from persons involved in the making of this policy (for example, Kerry, 2018: 424–9; Rodham Clinton, 2014: 222–8; Rhodes, 2019). Having said that, Obama's (first) autobiography *A Promised Land* (Obama, 2020) does not cover his Cuba policy.

Nonetheless, theory-driven explanations of said episode are few and far between. What is more, they also do not necessarily zoom in on, let alone theorize the role of President Obama in bringing about policy change in particular, as this book does. For example, Jacqueline Laguardia Martinez and colleagues (2020: 111–6, 126–8) include the perception that U.S.–Cuba policy failed to accomplish its goals as well as actions on part of Obama in their enumeration of factors that contributed to "positive change in Cuba-U.S. relations."[2] Yet they do not put forward a coherent framework that would allow isolating the specific impact of the president on this episode of policy change. In turn, one of the leading experts on U.S.–Cuban relations, William LeoGrande (2015b), explains the fundamental change in U.S.–Cuba policy by pointing to a set of structural factors, including threat environment, the role of the Cuban-American lobby in U.S. politics, Latin American views on the U.S.–Cuba antagonism, and developments within Cuba. He argues that concurrent changes in those factors presented Obama with the opportunity to introduce far-reaching policy changes. This structural account conceives Obama as essentially being driven to change U.S.–Cuba policy, rather than being the driver of said changes.[3] In another article, LeoGrande (2020) includes Obama's 2014 announcement to start an engagement policy with Cuba among a set of 13 decisions on U.S.–Cuba policy. However, in this case his interest lies specifically in exploring the role of the Cuban-American lobby in U.S.–Cuba policy rather than that of the U.S. president. In sum, there is a palpable gap in the theory-driven literature concerning the distinct role that President Obama might have had in bringing about a fundamental change in U.S. policy toward Cuba.[4]

Alternative explanatory factors

The main goal of this book is to introduce a new analytical framework to study major foreign policy change that places individual leaders front and center. However, as outlined earlier, the FPA literature on foreign policy change proposes numerous structural explanatory factors located on the domestic or international level as well. To explore whether a structural account offers an equally, or even more, convincing explanation for the empirical case under examination—in form of changes in U.S. foreign policy toward Cuba during the Obama administration—the book also briefly explores the case through three additional "non-leader" lenses that have been highlighted in the FPA literature.

A first alternative driver of foreign policy change results from *international pressure* on a country to change course. Such pressures can spring from many different sources (for example, Gustavsson, 1999: 83–5; Kleistra and Mayer, 2001: 392). For instance, more powerful states might push a country to redirect its foreign policy, thereby aligning it more closely to the interests of the great power. Further, high levels of interdependence among states might mean that changes in the policies of other states require adjustments in one's own policy. A similar effect can follow from changes in international norms to which a country must respond. Last but not least, Hermann (1990: 12) flags "external shocks," understood as "large events in terms of visibility and immediate impact on the recipient," as another external factor that puts pressure on a country to alter its foreign policy.

Building on a rich tradition in FPA (for example, Allison, 1971; Halperin, 1974; Allison and Zelikow, 1999), a second alternative driver highlights the role of *bureaucratic pressure* to change foreign policy. While organizational interests typically favor stability over change (Welch, 2005: 31–6), bureaucratic actors can nonetheless act as key change agents under certain conditions. Hermann (1990: 11) refers to this as "bureaucratic advocacy" where "a group within the government becomes an advocate of redirection." Hermann is agnostic as to whether the bureaucratic actors are placed in a single or in different organizations. Rather, key for bureaucratic actors' ability to act as change agents is that they are "sufficiently well placed to have some access to top officials" (Hermann, 1990: 12).

A final alternative driver of foreign policy change comes in form of *societal pressure*. Hence, within the domestic arena they key impetus for change is not provided by leaders nor by bureaucracies but by societal actors. Under the label "domestic restructuring," Hermann (1990: 12) refers to "the politically relevant segment of society whose support a regime needs to govern." Accordingly, "public opposition" (Doeser, 2011) and ensuing pressures for change can result, for example, when key constituencies of parties (for example, trade unions or business lobbies) or larger segments of society more broadly no longer support the continuation of certain policies (Kleistra and Mayer, 2001: 392). This puts pressure on leaders to change course. Otherwise, their chances of survival in office diminish.

Contributions of the volume

This volume seeks to contribute to the scholarly literature both theoretically and empirically. On the one hand, it seeks to advance the FPA literature on foreign policy change by proposing a "leader-centered theory of foreign policy change." As outlined before, there is clearly no dearth in scholarship on foreign policy change in general terms. However, while most works do ascribe "some" role to leaders in bringing about foreign policy change, they tend to be unspecific about the distinct role that leaders play in this regard. To that end, this book introduces a novel theory that seeks to ascertain whether leaders have an independent, systematic, and predictable effect on foreign policy change. In so doing, the volume also seeks to contribute to the public policy scholarship on policy change by heeding calls from said literature to integrate the concept of policy entrepreneurs in a broader framework of policy change (Mintrom and Norman, 2009: 663) and, building on this, to engage in "theory-driven, systematic empirical work" (Mintrom, 2020: 48) which "is needed to link policy entrepreneurs' characteristics and strategies" (Frisch Arivam et al, 2020: 630).

On the other hand, the volume seeks to add to the empirical literature on U.S. foreign policy toward Cuba during the Obama presidency. As outlined, this episode has received little attention so far particularly in terms of theory-driven accounts, which is surprising given how prominent an issue—both in terms of foreign policy and domestic politics—U.S.–Cuban relations have been for decades. In addition to this lacuna in theory-driven analyses, the so far sparse literature contains an empirical puzzle pertaining to the concrete role that President Obama played in bringing about a fundamental change in U.S.–Cuba policy.

There seems to be agreement that a realist, threat-oriented perspective is not particularly helpful in this case (LeoGrande, 2015b: 487). There is less agreement, however, in terms of what drove U.S. policy instead. Whether a confluence of changes in structural factors on the domestic level (in both the United States and Cuba) and the regional level (in Latin America) opened up a window of opportunity that Obama then used to usher in change, as proposed by LeoGrande (2015b: 488), offers a convincing explanation seems debatable. In the final analysis, such a structural argument would suggest that any president at that time would have initiated far-reaching changes in response to structural incentives. So had, for instance, Hillary Clinton won the Democratic presidential nomination in 2008 and later the presidential elections, or had respectively Republicans John McCain or Mitt Romney prevailed over Obama in the 2008 and 2012 presidential elections, fundamental change would have come as well. This seems rather questionable. Therefore, this book offers an alternative, leader-centered account of the episode of major changes in U.S. foreign policy toward Cuba during the Obama administration that seeks to complement existing structurally-oriented explanations.

Plan of the book

The remainder of this book contains four more parts. Chapter Two introduces the "leader-centered theory of foreign policy change." Chapter Three applies this theory to the case of U.S. foreign policy change toward Cuba during the Obama administration. Chapter Four examines whether alternative structural explanatory factors are capable of providing (similarly) convincing explanations of the U.S.–Cuba policy under Obama. Chapter Five concludes the discussion by summarizing the argument, briefly examining the Cuba policies of Obama's successor Donald Trump, and suggesting avenues for future research.

TWO

A Leader-Centered Theory of Foreign Policy Change

This chapter introduces a "leader-centered theory of foreign policy change." The theory seeks to account for the independent, systematic, and predictable effect of leaders in bringing about major changes in a country's foreign policy, in the sense of broader redirections that entail multiple decisions spanning different issue areas. More specifically, the theory explores the possible effect of leaders on the "why," the "what," and the "how" of foreign policy change in terms of:

- the reasons due to which leaders try to fundamentally redirect their countries' foreign policy, which is henceforth referred to as "triggering change";
- the substantive direction in which leaders seek to change foreign policy, which is henceforth referred to as "guiding change"; and
- the actions that leaders undertake to bring about change in the domestic political arena, which is henceforth referred to as "implementing change."

The theory is distinct from alternative explanatory frameworks in that it evolves around individual leaders and at the same time systemically incorporates insights from the public policy literature.

The first key feature of the theory is its explicit focus on leaders as key "change agents" (Hermann, 1990). Indeed, most analytical frameworks in Foreign Policy Analysis (FPA) that seek to account for foreign policy change bring together an array of structural and actor-oriented explanatory factors (for example, Holsti, 1982; Hermann, 1990; Rosati, 1994; Gustavsson, 1999; Welch, 2005; Blavoukos and Bourantonis, 2014; Joly and Haesebrouck, 2021; see also Chapter One of this volume). As a result, it is all but impossible to ascertain any independent and systematic effect that leaders might have on foreign policy change. The leader-centered theory outlined in this chapter offers an alternative perspective that conceptualizes individual decision makers as being crucial for the initiation, direction, and implementation of foreign policy change.

The second key feature is that the theory draws heavily on insights from the field of public policy. The first strand of literature that the theory incorporates is the one on policy failures (for example, Marsh and McConnell, 2010; Bovens and 't Hart, 2016; McConnell, 2016). This scholarship has so far received scant attention in FPA research. It offers a more nuanced and systematic conceptualization of the phenomenon of policy failure compared to what can be found in the extant FPA literature, which is why it is brought to bear in the leader-centered theory to account for leaders' diagnosis of policy failure. The second strand of public policy literature that is incorporated in the theory is the one on policy entrepreneurs (for example, Kingdon, 2011; Mintrom, 2000, 2020). From it, the theory distills different instruments and strategies that leaders can employ when pursuing and implementing policy change in the domestic political arena. While other FPA works have also drawn on this literature (for example, Carter and Scott, 2009; Lantis, 2019), the theory proposed in this book moves beyond those works by connecting insights from the literature on policy entrepreneurs with a leader-centered FPA theory, in the form of Leadership Trait Analysis (LTA). In so doing, the theory conceptualizes the selection of specific entrepreneurial instruments and strategies as a function of leaders' traits.

To be sure, although this theory places leaders front and center, this is not to suggest that structural factors, both international and domestic ones, are irrelevant or that leaders are detached from them (on the "agency-structure debate" in FPA, see, for example, Carlsnaes, 1992). However, arguing from a psychological perspective on foreign policy making, the assumption is that the broader effects as well as the more specific opportunities and constraints that spring from structural factors are not exogenously predetermined. Rather, they become meaningful only through leaders' perception and handling of them. Hence, the impact that structural factors have on foreign policy is a function of how they are perceived by decision makers and of the instruments and strategies that decision makers employ respectively to make use of the opportunities offered or to circumvent the constraints posed by structural factors.

In this sense, Harold and Margaret Sprout argued already several decades ago that "Environmental factors become related to the attitudes and decisions which, in the aggregate, comprise a state's foreign policy *only* by being apperceived and taken into account by those who participate in the policy-forming process" (Sprout and Sprout, 1957: 310, emphasis in the original). Similarly, Jakob Gustavsson (1999: 84) suggests that "it is not the objective reality that counts, but how this is perceived and reacted to by the decision-makers." More recently, Juliet Kaarbo (2019a: 35) stated in a discussion of what FPA scholarship can add to the broader International Relations (IR) literature that "attention to the micro-foundations is a necessary part of understanding international politics, given that macro-level dynamics and structures are filtered through and interpreted by individuals situated in domestic institutions and internal political systems." Arguing from a broader IR perspective, Goddard also draws attention on "the link between micro-action and macro-outcomes" (2009: 250) and suggests that "Structures might constrain agents, but entrepreneurs can remake and transform these structures, creating new institutions, contesting norms and values, and creating space for significant political change" (2009: 249).

The proposed leader-centered theory builds on those insights, which suggest not only that structures become meaningful primarily through how actors perceive them but also that actors are capable of overcoming structural constraints. From this vantage point, it zooms in on the micro-foundations of foreign policy change. The theory conceptualizes major foreign policy change and the role of leaders therein as the outcome of a three-stage process that entails "triggering change" (the "why" of foreign policy change), "guiding change" (the "what" foreign policy change), and "implementing change" (the "how" of foreign policy change). While the three stages are in effect interdependent, for analytical reasons they can be discussed separately since they cover distinct aspects of the change process.

Triggering change suggests that for leaders to invest political capital and undertake efforts to fundamentally reorient their country's foreign policy, they must first perceive the current policy as failing or as already having failed. It is here where the theory draws on insights from the public policy literature on policy failure to identify leaders' diagnoses of policy failure. *Guiding change* refers to the substantive direction in which leaders seek to redirect their country's foreign policy based on their diagnoses of policy failure. The theory argues that leaders' political beliefs guide their efforts in this regard. Operational Code Analysis (OCA) is used to identify leaders' beliefs and the ensuing direction of foreign policy change. Finally, *implementing change* focuses on how leaders seek to realize their proposed new course of foreign policy in the domestic political arena. Here, the theory brings together the public policy literature on policy entrepreneurs with LTA by suggesting that leaders' traits influence their choice of entrepreneurial instruments and strategies based on which they seek to put into practice the aspired policy redirection. Figure 2.1 presents an overview of the building blocks of the

A LEADER-CENTERED THEORY OF FOREIGN POLICY CHANGE

Figure 2.1: Analytical framework

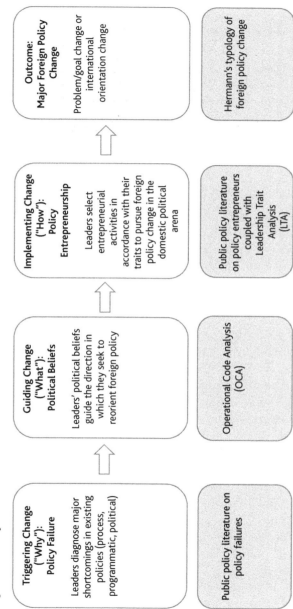

theory together with information on the scholarly literatures that the respective blocks build on.

The remainder of this chapter first discusses what is meant by "major" foreign policy change. The chapter then zooms in on the three elements of the leader-centered theory of foreign policy change, in form of "triggering change," "guiding change," and "implementing change." Next comes a discussion of methods and data. The chapter concludes with a brief summary.

Grasping change: major foreign policy changes

This book seeks to explain *major* redirections in a country's foreign policy. This presupposes that it is possible to distinguish between different types of change. Indeed, there is broad agreement in FPA scholarship that there is not just one monolithic type of foreign policy change but that differentiation is required. Accordingly, based on different cut-off points or spots on a continuum, the literature points to various types, levels, or degrees of change. To give but three examples:

Arguably the most prominent typology are Charles Hermann's "four graduated levels of change," which he calls "adjustment change," "program change," "problem/goal change," and "international orientation change" (Hermann, 1990). Jerel Rosati (1994) proposes a similar four-fold typology of foreign policy change that comprises "intensification," "refinement," "reform," and "restructuring." In turn, K.J. Holsti (1982) focuses exclusively on the most far-reaching type of change, which he also calls "restructuring" and which he breaks down into "isolation," "self-reliance," "dependence," and "non-alignment diversification."

While far from being irrelevant, the more minor types of foreign policy change are typically primarily technical in nature, thus less political than the more far-reaching ones. More often than not, decisions on such minor changes fall under the remit of bureaucratic actors. Conversely, the major types of foreign policy change have by definition much broader implications and are therefore also more political. It is in such non-routine and longer-range decisions where the political leaders of a country, such as prime ministers or presidents, are involved and, crucially for the argument presented in this volume, where their *influence is most likely to materialize* (Holsti, 1976: 30). A similar argument can be found in the public policy literature. For example, proponents of Punctuated Equilibrium Theory suggest that major policy changes occur only when issues move out of the expert-driven micro-level of politics, which is characterized by stasis or only incremental adjustments, and move up to the macro-level of politics, where political actors possibly enact far-reaching changes (for example, Baumgartner et al, 2017).

Accordingly, this book focuses on major episodes of foreign policy change and seeks to ascertain the role of high-ranking political leaders in such contexts. In terms of what qualifies as major foreign policy change, the argument draws on Hermann's typology in general and the two most far-reaching types of foreign policy change therein more specifically, namely problem/goal change and international orientation change respectively (Hermann, 1990: 5–6). Whereas problem/goal change encompasses changes in the purposes or goals that are associated with or pursued by a certain foreign policy, international orientation change comprises "the redirection of the actor's entire orientation toward world affairs" and "involves a basic shift in the actor's international role and activities." Accordingly, the implementation of international orientation change is not confined to one specific domain of foreign policy (for example, security or trade) but triggers changes in multiple domains at the same time.

In terms of ascertaining those types of foreign policy change, Hermann offers several suggestions with respect to the observable implications of problem/goal change and international orientation change respectively. Problem/goal change typically entails "changes in the configuration of instruments, in the level of commitment, and probably also in the degree of expressed affect." Further, it is accompanied by "policy statements and policy actions incompatible with prior goal or problem stipulations—if not open rejection of prior goals." In turn, international orientation change "involves dramatic changes in both words and deeds in multiple issue areas with respect to the actor's relationship with external entities" (all quotes from Hermann, 1990: 6).

Still, placing specific episodes within Hermann's typology remains challenging. In this sense, Hermann himself concedes that "Reliable empirical differentiation is not always easy" (Hermann, 1990: 6). The leader-centered theory on foreign policy change proposed in this volume cannot fix this problem. At the same time, I contend that this is not overly problematic for the overall argument. After all, the criteria set out by Hermann are sufficiently precise to distinguish with reasonable confidence *major* episodes of foreign policy change (which henceforth are referred to interchangeably as major changes, redirections, or reorientations) from more minor episodes of foreign policy change. What is more, the goal of the volume is not to come up with a novel conceptualization of major foreign policy change as such but rather to trace possible independent and systematic effects of leaders with respect to the occurrence of that outcome. Thus, this book will refer to major foreign policy changes when several of the aforementioned indicators of either problem/goal or international orientation change can be identified.

Triggering change: major policy failure

The FPA and the public policy literatures feature a variety of expressions that are used more or less interchangeably to denote "policies gone wrong," including: "failure," "blunder," "mistake," or "fiasco" (see, for example, Janis, 1982; Gray and 't Hart, 1998; Bovens et al, 2001a; McConnell, 2010; Walker and Malici, 2011; Bovens and 't Hart, 2016; Jennings et al, 2018;

Kruck et al, 2018). Notwithstanding the specific term: The theory proposed in this volume argues that foreign policy change starts with foreign policy failure. That is, leaders must consider a current policy as exhibiting significant shortcomings in order to usher in a fundamental redirection of their country's foreign policy. Conversely, if a leader were to staunchly criticize a policy just for tactical reasons to gain short-term political gains without, however, actually considering the policy a major failure, there would be no need to fundamentally redirect policy in practice.

Major shortcomings exist when policies are perceived as having failed to bring about the aspired results now or as being unlikely to realize the country's goals in the future, or both. Policy failure can spring from different sources. For instance, a policy could have been ill-designed from the outset, which is why it was never likely to accomplish its objectives in the first place. Alternatively, changing circumstances can render obsolete a policy that was initially sound. Actions by third parties who start to actively challenge a policy can similarly lead to increasingly negative assessments of said policy. Irrespective of the specific reason or reasons as to why a policy is failing or has already failed in the eyes of a leader, the key point for the following discussion is that leaders *publicly decry a policy as major failure that is in need of substantial overhaul*. Such assessments indicate where leaders' political priorities lie. In addition, public statements put pressure on leaders to act on their critique by investing political capital in order to redirect their countries' foreign policy, thus following up words with deeds.

Whether leaders perceive major shortcomings in an existing policy prior to assuming office (for example, as a member of the political opposition who criticizes the policy of the incumbent government) or during office (for example, when having to cope with a major crisis that a policy has triggered) is irrelevant for the following argument. Indeed, major foreign policy change can be either the result of government turnover or initiated by a sitting leader. The key points are that a policy is labeled as a major failure and that leaders seek to remedy this shortcoming when having the opportunity to do so. Policy failures thus open up "windows of opportunity" that leaders can exploit to advance their policy agenda (Kingdon, 2011).

The connection between policy failure and foreign policy change has already been made in the FPA literature. For instance, Hermann (1990: 12–13) suggests that failure is a key driver for policy learning and ensuing policy change. In a later project, Hermann (2012b) also connects "what we do when things go wrong" and policy change. Similarly, Welch (2005: 46) highlights that decision makers associate "painful costs" with inaction, in the sense of continuing with an unsatisfactory policy, from which the need to foreign policy change arises.[1] However, the FPA literature on foreign policy change tends to be vague on how leaders go about determining *whether and, if so, in which regards* policies have actually failed. Public policy scholarship can help remedying this shortcoming since it offers a more fine-grained conceptualization of policy failure.

The public policy literature on (domestic) policy failures suggests that leaders evaluate policies along three dimensions, namely: programmatic, process, and political (Bovens et al, 2001b; Marsh and McConnell, 2010; McConnell, 2016). The *programmatic* dimension emphasizes the performative, problem-solving dimension of policy making. It explores whether a policy has offered an effective and efficient response to the policy challenge that it was supposed to address. Thus, it is ascertained whether a policy was implemented according to its objectives, whether resources have been used efficiently, and whether the eventual outcome was as intended (Marsh and McConnell, 2010: 571).

In turn, the *process* dimension zooms in on the making of a policy. Arguably the most relevant aspect in this regard concerns the legitimacy of the decision-making process, that is, whether policies are "produced through constitutional and quasi-constitutional procedures" (Marsh and McConnell,

2010: 572). In addition, the level of support that a policy has received during this process is of relevance. This concerns whether it met resistance within the government's or governing coalition's own ranks, whether it attracted support from the political opposition, and whether it garnered support among core constituencies outside of parliament (for example, interest groups or the media) (Marsh and McConnell, 2010: 571).

Finally, the *political* dimension shifts focus to the reputational as well as perceptual and discursive aspects of policy making. Accordingly, and contrary to other two dimensions which seek to ascertain objective "facts" associated with the making and implementation of policies, this dimension emphasizes the constructed and often times contested nature of policy evaluations (Bovens and 't Hart, 2016). Thus, the key question is how policies "are represented and evaluated in the political arena" (Bovens et al, 2001: 20). Following from typically very negative presentations and depictions of policies in the political discourse, this dimension boils down to the question of whether a policy has increased or decreased the standing and popularity of the actors who signed responsible for it, and ultimately their chances for political survival in office (Marsh and McConnell, 2010: 571).

In accordance with a leader-centered perspective, the diagnosis function evolves around the assessment of a policy by individual leaders who act as change agents. That is, a policy has failed when leaders perceive significant shortcomings in existing policies along one or more of the aforementioned dimensions (programmatic, process, political). Acting on such a diagnosis, leaders seek to redirect their countries' foreign policy. Further impetus to alter course can come from negative assessments of a given policy put forward by politicians from the leader's own party or from members of the governing coalition, among others. Ascriptions of failure to a policy by the broader public, as evidenced for instance by media reports or opinion polls, can have the same effect. Such assessments would support leaders' own policy evaluation in programmatic terms.

In addition, they could reinforce the political dimension in that they point to the benefits that could arise from addressing the shortcomings of a contested and seemingly unpopular policy.

Still, while assessments of failure by others can lend additional support and urgency to altering a policy, I contend that the main impetus for change emanates from the leader's own negative assessment of said policy. After all, myriad examples have shown that leaders can and do stubbornly cling to a policy that they deem appropriate despite significant pushback from both inside and outside government. Thus, it is first and foremost leaders' own negative diagnosis of an existing policy that makes them seek to redirect their countries' foreign policy.

Guiding change: political beliefs

Acting on a negative assessment of an existing policy, leaders seek to develop a new policy that aims at overcoming the deficiencies of the current one and that ultimately realizes the foreign policy objectives of their country. However, policies can be adjusted in many different ways. Thus, the question is in which direction leaders will seek to redirect their countries' foreign policy. The proposed leader-centered theory of foreign policy change suggests that political beliefs of leaders provide an answer to this question.

True, political beliefs, and differences therein between leaders, can also be of relevance in terms of the negative evaluation of policies. However, such assessments can be motivated by a variety of other reasons as well, including instrumental ones such as political maneuvering. Moreover, differences in the beliefs of leaders do not automatically translate into ascriptions of major failure to each and every policy. Thus, while beliefs may or may not play a role for critiquing a policy as major failure, I contend that they always do play a role when it comes to devising alternative policies that should replace the one that is deemed a major failure. It is therefore that political beliefs are placed front and center only in this discussion on "guiding change" rather than already in the preceding discussion on "triggering change."

Similarly, it is beyond the scope of this volume to ascertain why leaders have the beliefs that they have, which, by the way, is something that OCA scholarship in general has spent little time contemplating (Brummer and Oppermann, 2024: 226). It might even be the case that policy failures not only open up windows of opportunity for leaders to redirect a country's foreign policy in accordance with their beliefs but that policy failures lead to changes in leader's beliefs in the first place based on which they start seeking to reorient policy. This connection between policy failure, policy learning, and policy change is prominently discussed in the public policy literature (for example, May, 1992; Howlett, 2012; Dunlop et al, 2020). However, for the following argument it is not important why or for how long leaders exhibit certain beliefs. Rather, the key point is that it is the beliefs which leaders have with respect to a specific policy domain that guide the substantive direction in which they subsequently seek to reorient their country's foreign policy.

Indeed, when seeking to chart an alternative path of action leaders must take into consideration a variety of factors, and it is their political beliefs that serve as the key yardstick and reference point in this regard. In this sense, Spyros Blavoukos and Dimitris Bourantonis (2012: 602–3) argue that leaders' "preference for change and the drive of their policy differentiation originate from a different understanding, conceptualization and prioritization of international challenges, stemming fundamentally from their belief systems, cognitive factors and other idiosyncratic features." To be clear, the claim here is not that political beliefs determine every single foreign policy decision. Rather, the argument is that beliefs steer the overall direction in which a major reorientation of a country's foreign policy unfolds, which, as stated before, is not confined to a single decision but leads to adjustments across a whole set of issues. Similarly, the argument is not that political beliefs are of relevance only in the context of redirections of foreign policy. This is just the function of beliefs that the proposed theory is interested in.

The proposed leader-centered theory uses OCA to ascertain leaders' political beliefs (Leites, 1951; George, 1969; Schafer and Walker, 2006a, 2021). Arguing from a cognitive perspective, 'operational codes'—which arguably represents a rather misleading label for political beliefs—are defined as "a set of general beliefs about fundamental issues of history and central questions of politics as these bear, in turn, on the problem of action" (George, 1969: 191). Based on the specific manifestations of leaders' beliefs it is possible to draw interferences about the general direction in which leaders seek to redirect their countries' foreign policy. This is because OCA conceptualizes political beliefs "as causal mechanisms with steering effects" (Walker and Schafer, 2006: 7). Most importantly, political beliefs will provide information on whether leaders will redirect their countries' foreign policy in more conflictual or more cooperative directions.

More specifically, OCA comprises ten beliefs that are grouped into two clusters. Those are philosophical beliefs and instrumental beliefs respectively (see Table 2.1). Philosophical beliefs refer to decision makers' assumptions concerning the fundamental nature of politics. Most importantly, they concern whether the "the political universe [is] essentially one of harmony or conflict" (George, 1969: 201). Philosophical beliefs are thus crucial for the definition of a situation. It is "through" them that leaders apperceive and take into account the structural political environment within which they operate. The most important philosophical belief is P-1 (one of two "master beliefs"), which refers to a leader's perception of the "nature of the political universe," that is, the extent to which the political environment is considered hostile or friendly.

Conversely, instrumental beliefs relate to decision makers' understanding about ends-means relationships regarding action in the political realm. Crucially, they provide answers

Table 2.1: Philosophical and instrumental beliefs in Operational Code Analysis

Philosophical beliefs	Instrumental beliefs
P-1 What is the "essential" nature of political life? Is the political universe essentially one of harmony or conflict? What is the fundamental character of one's political opponents?	*I-1 What is the best approach for selecting goals or objectives for political action?*
P-2 What are the prospects for the eventual realization of one's fundamental political values and aspirations? Can one be optimistic, or must one be pessimistic on this score; and in what respects the one and/or the other?	I-2 How are the goals of action pursued most effectively?
P-3 Is the political future predictable? In what sense and to what extent?	I-3 How are the risks of political action calculated, controlled, and accepted?
P-4 How much "control" or "mastery" can one have over historical development? What is one's role in "moving" and "shaping" history in the desired direction?	I-4 What is the best "timing" of action to advance one's interest?
P-5 What is the role of "chance" in human affairs and in historical development?	I-5 What is the utility and role of different means for advancing one's interests?

Note: Master beliefs in italics

Source: Own depiction based on George (1969)

to the question "What is the best approach for selecting goals or objectives for political action?" (George, 1969: 205). Instrumental beliefs are thus decisive for the selection of the appropriate responses or instruments for the situation at hand. The most important instrumental belief is I-1 (the other "master belief" next to P-1), which refers to a leader's "strategic approach to goals," that is, whether he or she considers conflictual or cooperative strategies as more promising in the pursuit of policy goals.

OCA is a tried and tested tool to ascertain the political beliefs of leaders. It has been applied in multiple empirical studies, covering leaders from both Western (for example, Walker et al,

1998; Renshon, 2008; 2009; Brummer, 2016; Macdonald and Schneider, 2017; Özdamar and Ceydilek, 2020; Rabini et al, 2020a) and non-Western (for example, Malici and Malici, 2005; Feng, 2006; He and Feng, 2013; Dyson and Raleigh, 2014; Özdamar, 2017; Dyson and Parent, 2018; Özdamar and Canbolat, 2018; Conley, 2019) countries. For instance, comparative studies have demonstrated that leaders differ in systematic ways along their philosophical or instrumental beliefs (for example, Walker et al, 1999; He and Feng, 2015), with philosophical beliefs being seemingly more amenable to changes than instrumental ones (Renshon, 2008: 827). Further, studies have shown that the beliefs of individual decision makers have changed over time, for example, in response to major changes in the political environment, such as an external shock. In this regard, Walker and Schafer (2000) highlight that U.S. president Lyndon B. Johnson's beliefs changed during the escalation of a military conflict (that is, Vietnam) and Renshon (2008) shows that the beliefs of George W. Bush changed after 9/11. Last but not least, empirical studies have demonstrated that leaders exhibit different sets of beliefs for specific issue areas (for example, Walker and Schafer, 2000; Rabini et al, 2020b: 169–77). The key takeaways of this brief overview of OCA scholarship for this volume are that it is possible to systemically ascertain as well as compare the beliefs of leaders and that rather than seeking to come up with generic profiles of leaders for foreign policy as a whole, it is necessary to develop targeted, issue-specific profiles.

In short, there is ample evidence that OCA is a viable tool for determining political beliefs, and specific manifestations therein, of individual leaders. How OCA profiles are constructed is discussed later. Once a leader's OCA profile is in hand, the ensuing questions are how to interpret leaders' political beliefs and, more specifically, how to infer the new foreign policy direction in which a leader is likely to reorient a country's foreign policy given his or her set of political beliefs.

One way to make the political beliefs of the leader under examination meaningful in terms of inferring expectations with respect to the likely substantive redirection of policy is to compare this leader's profile with the profile of his or her predecessor—provided that the latter is held responsible for the failed policy by the leader under examination. Alternatively, one could, for example, compare the political beliefs of the same leader before and after an external shock. Any differences in beliefs that come to the fore based on such comparisons should provide specific indications regarding the direction into which a country's foreign policy will be changed. This is the case because differences in beliefs are connected to specific behavioral expectations.

In substantive terms, the key theme that emerges is one of cooperation or conflict. This is highlighted by the two aforementioned master beliefs contained in OCA. Those place emphasis on the level of cooperation or conflict that leaders diagnose in their political environment (P-1) on the one hand and the promise they ascribe to cooperative or conflictual strategies respectively in the pursuit of their political goals (I-1) on the other. The two master beliefs can also be used to illustrate the proposed connection between beliefs and behavior. For instance, if the leader under examination has a much higher P-1 score than his or her predecessor, the expectation would be that this leader perceives the political environment and the actors therein as considerably more friendly, trustworthy, and benign. This, in turn, should be mirrored in a more open, friendly, and cooperative approach of the leader toward the "other side" compared to his or her predecessor, and vice versa. Similarly, if the leader under examination has a much lower I-1 score than his or her predecessor, the expectation would be that this leader sees greater merit in conflictual strategies and therefore places more emphasis on them when redirecting foreign policy, and vice versa.

Connections between specific manifestations of individual beliefs and expected behavior can be established for all OCA beliefs (see Table 2.2). It is those differences in leaders' beliefs that should inform the direction in which a leader reorients his or her country's foreign policy in response to a diagnosis of policy failure.[2]

Table 2.2: Behavioral implications of political beliefs

	Political belief	**Manifestation**	**Behavioral expectation**
P-1	Nature of the Political Universe	Friendly, mixed, hostile	The lower the value, the more hostile other actors ("Others") are perceived; the higher the value, the more friendly other actors ("Others") are perceived.
P-2	Realization of Political Values	Optimism versus pessimism	The lower the value, the more pessimistic the prospects for implementing goals are assessed; the higher the value, the more optimistic the prospects for implementing goals are assessed.
P-3	Predictability of Political Future	Low to high	The lower the value, the less predictable the political universe appears; the higher the value, the more predictable the political universe appears.
P-4	Control over Historical Development	Low to high	The lower the value, the more control is assigned to "Others;" the higher the value, the more control is assigned to "Self."
P-5	Role of Chance	Low to high	The less predictable the political universe (P-3) and the less control over developments (P-4) appear, the greater the role of chance; the more predictable the political universe (P-3) and the greater control over developments (P-4) appear, the smaller the role of chance.

Table 2.2: Behavioral implications of political beliefs (continued)

	Political belief	Manifestation	Behavioral expectation
I-1	Strategic Approach to Goals	Cooperation, mixed, conflictual	The lower the value, the greater the benefit assigned to conflictive strategies; the higher the value, the greater the benefit assigned to cooperative strategies.
I-2	Tactical Pursuit of Goals	Cooperation, mixed, conflictual	The lower the value, the greater the benefit assigned to enemy tactics; the higher the value, the greater the benefit assigned to cooperative tactics.
I-3	Risk Orientation	Averse to acceptant	The lower the value, the lower the willingness to take risks; the higher the value, the higher the willingness to take risks.
I-4	Timing of Action a. cooperation/ conflict b. words/ deeds	Low to high flexibility	The lower the value, the less flexible decision makers are in selecting their instruments; the higher the value, the more flexible decision makers are in selecting their instruments.
I-5	Utility of Means a. reward b. promise c. appeal d. oppose e. threaten f. punish	Low to high	The lower the share of a verb category (reward, promise, and so on), the lower the utility of the respective instrument is rated; the larger the share of a verb category (reward, promise, and so on), the higher the utility of the respective instrument is rated.

Source: Own depiction based on Walker and Schafer (2006b: 32–8)

Implementing change: policy entrepreneurship

The preceding sections have conceptualized leaders' diagnosis of a fundamentally flawed policy as the trigger of foreign policy change and leaders' political beliefs as the key substantive drivers in terms of the direction in which policy should change. The remaining question is how leaders seek to bring about foreign policy change in the domestic political arena. Indeed, for foreign policy change to occur it is not sufficient to solely criticize existing policy and propose alternatives to it. In this sense, Michael Mintrom and Joannah Luetjens (2018: 397) suggest that "All proposals for policy change must gain support and legitimacy within relevant institutional settings." In a similar vein, Charles-Philippe David (2015: 168) argues that "The ideational goals behind the decision cannot be realized unless support for them can be garnered within the decision-making system." Therefore, the third and final stage of the leader-centered theory addresses the implementation of the new policy in the domestic political arena. It is here where political entrepreneurs employ social skills as well as structural mechanisms in the pursuit of policy change. Drawing on insights from both the public policy literature and the FPA literature, the leader-centered theory conceives leaders as policy entrepreneurs whose choice of entrepreneurial instruments and strategies is guided by their leadership traits. The following discussion first zooms in on the concept of policy entrepreneurs, then introduces LTA, and finally suggests how leadership traits influence leaders' actions as policy entrepreneurs through which they seek to put into practice a change in policy.

Policy entrepreneurs

The concept of policy entrepreneurs is prominently discussed in the public policy literature (for example, Roberts and King, 1991; King and Roberts, 1992; Schneider and Teske, 1992;

Mintrom, 2000; Mintrom and Norman, 2009; Kingdon, 2011; Cairney, 2018; Mintrom, 2020; Petridou and Mintrom, 2021). The concept has also already been applied to the realm of foreign policy (for example, Mazarr, 2007; Carter and Scott, 2009; Blavoukos and Bourantonis, 2012; David, 2015; Macdonald, 2015; Marsh and Lantis, 2018; Mintrom and Luetjens, 2018; Lantis, 2019). This volume's leader-centered theory of foreign policy change contributes to the latter discussion by coupling it with insights from the FPA literature. Importantly, the goal associated with the use of the policy entrepreneur concept is not to ascertain whether a leader has acted in such a role or not. Rather, the goal is to discuss what leaders do when they act as policy entrepreneur and to explore why they prefer certain entrepreneurial instruments or strategies over others. In other words, the discussion does not seek to explore the conditions (structural context or personal attributes) under which a leader becomes a policy entrepreneur, nor whether there are systematic differences in policy entrepreneurship depending on who acts in this capacity (leaders, bureaucrats, and so on) but rather takes entrepreneurial action by a political leader from the executive branch as its point of departure. This follows Mintrom and Luetjens (2018: 397) who suggest that policy entrepreneurship is not per se restricted to advisors, bureaucrats, parliamentarians, or experts but can also be fulfilled by "designated political leaders—presidents, foreign ministers, or secretaries of state."[3]

Hence, the goal is to explain how leaders who use their "office as a base from which to engage in policy entrepreneurship" (Mintrom and Luetjens, 2018: 397) try to bring about policy change in practice. To that end, the leader-centered theory draws on FPA's LTA. It suggests that specific manifestations of leadership traits render the use of certain policy entrepreneurial instruments and strategies more likely than others, thus offering systematic insights on how leaders who act as policy entrepreneurs seek to implement foreign policy change in the domestic political arena. This approach mirrors in principle the one adopted by Neomi Frisch Aviram and colleagues (2020) who also connect personal attributes of policy entrepreneurs with the strategies that they employ. However, those authors base their study on other entrepreneurial strategies and leader attributes than those used in this volume.

The concept of policy entrepreneurs aligns nicely with this volume's goal of explaining major (foreign) policy change with a focus on leaders for several reasons. First, the concept obviously places the agency of individual actors front and center, as does this book. Arguably the most prominent characterization of policy entrepreneurs has been developed by John Kingdon who suggested that

> their defining characteristic ... is their willingness to invest their resources—time, energy, reputation, and sometimes money—in the hope of a future return. That return might come to them in the form of policies of which they approve, satisfaction from participation, or even personal aggrandizement in the form of job security or career promotion. (Kingdon, 2011: 122–3)

Thus, alterations to existing policy—on which this book focuses on—is one of the possible "future returns" which drive policy entrepreneurs. In this sense, the latter have been labeled "agents of policy change" (Mintrom and Luetjens, 2019: 113) whose actions "disrupt the status quo" (Mintrom, 2020: 10).

Second, policy entrepreneurs are intimately associated not only with policy change per se, as already indicated, but with far-reaching policy change in particular. In this sense, policy entrepreneurs often times advance new ideas that, if implemented, "significantly change current ways of doing things in their area of interest" (Mintrom and Norman, 2009: 650). Importantly, the literature on policy entrepreneurs does not restrict the measure of impact, thus change, to legislative change. Rather, it also acknowledges "broader policy adjustments" or "broad system change" (Mintrom et al, 2020: 6, 8) beyond the realm of legislation as evidence for policy change. This is highly relevant for the purpose of this book since foreign policy is for the most part not governed by formal legislation but grounded in leaders' statements, policy documents, nonbinding declarations, bi- or multilateral agreements, and so on.

Finally, activities by policy entrepreneurs are supposed to occur in particular contexts, such as political crises or policy failures (for example, Mintrom and Norman, 2009: 652; Navot and Cohen, 2015: 65; Mintrom et al, 2020: 13). The latter is also the point of departure of the proposed leader-centered theory. Policy failures open up policy windows that entrepreneurs can exploit in their pursuit of altering their country's policy. As Michael Mintrom and Phillipa Norman (2009: 650) argue:

> The extant literature suggests that policy entrepreneurship is most likely to be observed in cases where change involves disruption to established ways of doing things … [I]nstances occur when new challenges appear so significant that established systems of managing them are judged inadequate. A key part of policy entrepreneurship involves seizing such moments to promote major change.

Overall, then, leaders who seek to fundamentally redirect their country's course of action in response to perceived policy failure can be considered policy entrepreneurs. The ensuing question concerns the instruments and strategies that policy entrepreneurs employ in their effort to implement policy change in the domestic political arena. The public policy literature puts forward an array of actions that policy entrepreneurs might undertake in this regard (for example, Roberts and King, 1991; Faling et al, 2019; Frisch Aviram et al, 2020; Mintrom, 2020). Importantly, the assumption is not that all policy entrepreneurs place identical emphasis on the various tools at their disposal in bringing about major policy change. Rather, depending on the political context and their own predispositions and capabilities, we should expect to see variation with respect to the instruments and strategies that leaders employ when acting as policy entrepreneurs (Mintrom, 2020: 13). While leaders typically combine different instruments and strategies, their entrepreneurial activities can focus more on collective efforts or instead place greater emphasis on their own person.

The following discussion covers many but not all of the strategies and instruments that can be found in the diverse literature on policy entrepreneurs. Arguably the most important omission relates to the "framing of problems" (Mintrom, 2020: 14–15). While clearly of importance, such efforts in terms of problem definition/representation and sense-making more generally are not considered in the following discussion since the leader-centered theory addresses this activity already in its two previous stages, first when identifying and describing the problem during the "triggering change" stage and then when proposing substantive solutions during the "guiding change" stage. This third stage ("implementing change") focuses on the *political maneuvering* that is associated with bringing about policy change. The following discussion highlights four entrepreneurial instruments and strategies that leaders could employ to that effect, with the first one placing emphasis on group-oriented actions while the others emphasizing more the role of the individual leader him- or herself.

One instrument is *team building*. While a leader who acts as policy entrepreneur is the driving force behind the effort to redirect policy, the assumption is that he or she cannot accomplish that goal singlehandedly. Rather, a leader connects with other actors in order to increase his or her leverage. As Mintrom and Norman (2009: 653) suggest: "Individuals are often the instigators of change, but their strength does not come from the force of their ideas alone, or from their embodiment of superhuman qualities. Rather, their real strength comes through their ability to work effectively with others."

Efforts of policy entrepreneurs toward team building can be broken down into three distinct variants. The first concerns the creation of a core group or "tight-knit team" (Mintrom, 2020: 16) that the leader employs to drive the process of change forward. The members of that group support the leader in many different ways, such as offering information and advice, acting as conduits, and providing political support more broadly. The second variant pertains to a leader making use of his or her broader professional and/or private networks in the pursuit of policy change. Those networks also provide information and support. The networks that a leader has inside the political arena are considered particularly relevant "for actually making change happen" (Mintrom, 2020: 17). The third variant concerns a leader's interaction with advocacy coalitions. Advocacy coalition are groups of people who hold shared beliefs and seek to influence policy making in accordance with those ("policy core" and "deep core") beliefs (Weible et al, 2020). A leader who acts as policy entrepreneur can either create new or work with existing advocacy coalitions with the goal of enhancing the credibility of his or her substantive goals. In addition, composition and size of the group can lend political support to the leader's cause.

Another instrument is *leading by example*. This occurs when leaders "tak[e] an idea and turn[] it into action themselves" (Mintrom, 2020: 19). This could entail both verbal and physical "actions." Thus, when leading by example, a leader can, for example, make certain proclamations or engage in symbolic actions (gestures, visits, and so on) that signal his or her commitment to the proposed course of action (here: policy change), which in turn enhances the credibility of the leader and of his or her policy goal with others. Conversely, a leader can also make a statement by refraining to repeat certain commitments or to engage in certain activities. Either way, such actions "prefigure and lay the groundwork for subsequent broad-based change" (Mintrom, 2020: 43). In addition, they can also catch opponents of policy change off-guard, putting them on the defensive and diminishing the credibility of their claims in favor of policy stability.

Moreover, a leader can *scale-up advocacy efforts* in order to support policy change. This activity emphasizes how important the sequence and right order of action are in bringing about policy change. Thus, a leader first has to select the right point of entry and then has to continuously expand the scope of his or her activities and support base. It is through well-timed and "well-chosen actions" (Mintrom and Luetjens, 2018: 402) that a leader seeks to maintain the momentum for policy change.

A final area of action concerns the *transformation of institutions*. The expectation is that a leader who acts as policy entrepreneur not only has an intimate knowledge of the institutional environment within which he or she is operating. In addition, a leader actively tries to manipulate the given institutional set-up in his or her favor. The underlying goal is "to alter the distribution of authority and power and/or transform existing institutions" (Faling et al, 2019: 405) in order to increase the likelihood of introducing major policy change. This can be accomplished, for example, by increasing the representation of the leader's supporters in key institutions or by bypassing established channels of action that might pose challenges to their change effort (Meijerink and Huitema, 2010).

Leadership Trait Analysis

After outlining key instruments and strategies that leaders who act as policy entrepreneurs can employ to bring about major (foreign) policy change, the ensuing question is what drives leaders' choices in this regard in the first place. Thus, why do leaders focus more on certain instruments and strategies than on others? For that purpose, the leader-centered theory draws on LTA (Hermann, 1980a, 1984, 2005a; Hermann et al, 2001). It suggests that specific manifestations of leaders' traits can be systematically connected to the selection of policy entrepreneurial instruments and strategies that leaders take up in their pursuit of foreign policy change. The discussion first introduces LTA and then shows how policy entrepreneurial actions and leaders' traits are linked.

Like OCA just discussed, LTA also belongs to the at-a-distance assessment techniques for profiling political leaders. The main proponent of LTA defines leadership style as "the ways in which leaders relate to those around them—whether constituents, advisers, or other leaders—and how they structure interactions and the norms, rules, and principles they use to guide such interactions" (Hermann, 2005a: 181). Hence, a specific leadership style, as well as the distinct leadership traits out of which a specific leadership style emerges, exert a significant impact on the way that leaders seek to cope with the challenges and dilemmas of foreign policy making. While LTA's focus is on individual leaders, this is not say that structural factors are irrelevant. However, the argument is that leaders perceive and respond to structural opportunities and constraints differently. For example, while some leaders challenge constraints, others respect them. Following from this, how leaders navigate the political arena and, more specifically, which instruments and strategies they employ in the pursuit of policy change is a function of leaders' characteristics, in form of leadership traits.

LTA evolves around seven distinct leadership traits. Those are:

- *belief in the ability to control events* (BACE): leaders' perception of having control and influence over situations and developments;
- *need for power* (PWR): leaders' aspiration to control, influence, or impact other actors;
- *conceptual complexity* (CC): leaders' ability to differentiate things and people in their environment;
- *self-confidence* (SC): leaders' sense of self-importance as well as perceived ability to cope with their environment;

- *task focus* (TASK): whether leaders focus on problem solving or group maintenance/relationships;
- *distrust of others* (DIS): leaders' tendency to suspect or doubt the motives and deeds of others; and
- *in-group bias* (IGB): leaders' tendency to value (socially, politically, and so on defined) group and place the group front and center.

Those seven traits can be interacted to produce eight "leadership styles" (Hermann, 2005a). However, like most LTA studies, this volume focuses on traits rather than styles. In addition to practical reasons that can turn the aggregation of the individual traits into overarching styles challenging (Brummer, 2023: 244–5), the use of traits rather than styles allows to develop more specific connections with leaders' propensities to prefer certain entrepreneurial instruments and strategies over others.

LTA has been employed in numerous empirical studies which covered leaders from both Western (for example, Hermann, 2005b; Keller, 2005; Dyson, 2006, 2007; Yang, 2010; Van Esch and Swinkels, 2015; Dyson, 2018; Keller et al, 2020) and non-Western (for example, Hermann, 1980b; Taysi and Preston, 2001; Hermann, 2005c; Kesgin, 2013; Cuhadar et al, 2017; Kesgin, 2020; Fouquet and Brummer, 2023) countries. Among other things, the empirical studies have demonstrated that leaders' traits remain essentially stable (though not static) over time, even after changing positions in government (Cuhadar et al, 2017; Rabini et al, 2020a). Further, traits have been connected to a range of foreign policy behaviors and outcomes, including diversionary behavior (Keller and Foster, 2012) and foreign policy fiascos (Brummer, 2016).

In short, LTA is a viable tool for determining leaders' traits. It focuses on the way leaders relate to and interact with their environment rather than on the substantive direction of policies. Therefore, it is not used in the "guiding phase" of the leader-centered theory. True, LTA can and already has been employed to explain leaders' propensity to enact foreign policy change. Focusing on the trait "conceptual complexity," Yi Edward Yang (2010) found that leaders with a high manifestation in that trait are more likely to redirect foreign policy than low-complexity leaders and also that the latter require stronger stimuli to engage in that activity.[4] However, since the proposed leader-centered theory starts in the "triggering phase" with the diagnosis of major policy failure, the latter can be seen as qualifying as major stimulus based on which both high- and low-complexity leaders are likely to enact change. Against this background, this project uses LTA in a more targeted fashion by connecting traits and policy entrepreneurial actions. How leaders' LTA profiles are constructed is shown in the section on "Methods and data." The discussion now turns to question of how to infer leaders' preferences for certain policy entrepreneurial instruments and strategies based on their traits.

Choosing entrepreneurial instruments and strategies

The leader-centered theory suggests that certain leadership traits can be connected to specific entrepreneurial instruments and strategies and, following from this, that specific manifestations of traits offer indications as to which of those instruments and strategies a leader places particular, or for that matter limited, emphasis on, thus employs to a larger or lesser extent. As outlined, the analytical framework focuses on four types of policy entrepreneurial actions: team building, leading by example, scaling-up the advocacy efforts, and transforming institutions. Although there might be additional connections between entrepreneurial actions and leaders' traits, the following appear the most straightforward (see also Table 2.3):

- Whether a leader *builds and works through teams* can be tied to TASK, DIS, and IGB respectively. Leaders with a low

A LEADER-CENTERED THEORY OF FOREIGN POLICY CHANGE

Table 2.3: Policy entrepreneurial actions and leadership traits

Policy entrepreneurial instruments and strategies	Leadership trait(s)	Expectation
Team building (core groups; networks; advocacy coalitions)	Task focus (TASK); distrust of others (DIS); in-group bias (IGB)	Low TASK should render team-building more likely. High DIS should restrict team-building efforts to use of core groups and networks. High IGB should restrict team-building efforts to use of core groups and networks.
Leading by example	Self-confidence (SC); belief in the ability to control events (BACE)	High SC makes use more likely. High BACE makes use more likely.
Scaling up advocacy efforts	Conceptual complexity (CC)	High CC makes use more likely.
Transforming institutions	Need for power (PWR)	High PWR makes use more likely.

task focus place emphasis on group building and group maintenance rather than problem solving and should therefore devote more attention to team building in general terms. In turn, a high level of distrust of others should restrict leaders' team-building efforts to core groups from within his or her networks but not to a broader set of people. A similar effect can be expected if a leader exhibits a strong in-group bias, based on which he or she might shy away from broadening support for policy change by reaching out to "out-groups."

- *Leading by example* can be connected to SC and BACE, respectively. Leaders with high manifestations in those traits should be particularly likely to engage in high-profile and maybe even risky actions, thereby signaling commitment to their proposed course of policy change.
- Leaders' ability and willingness to *scale-up advocacy efforts* to bring about policy change can be linked to CC. As outlined, the former emphasizes the importance of the right sequence of action in bringing about foreign policy change. Leaders with a high level of conceptual complexity, thus cognitive ability, should be particularly prone and capable to employ this instrument. That is, based on their ability to perceive nuances of situations and contexts, such leaders are particularly able to recognize situations where additional impetus is required to move the process of policy change forward, and act accordingly.
- Finally, efforts to *transform institutions* can spring from leaders' PWR. Leaders with a high manifestation of that trait should place particular emphasis on manipulating the institutional set-up in their favor. This would not only render foreign policy change more likely as such but also increase the leeway and leverage that the individual leader holds over that process in the first place, thereby diminishing the need to coordinate or even compromise with other actors.

The preceding discussion has referred throughout to "high" or "low" manifestations of certain leadership traits. The ensuing final question is how high or low manifestations of a trait can be ascertained in the first place. To do this, LTA provides a "norming group." This group contains close to 300 decision makers from around the world. This group has also been broken down into several, mostly geographically defined sub-groups, such as Western Europe, Pacific Rim, and Anglo-America. Average trait scores for the seven traits captured by LTA are provided for the entire norming group as well as for the respective sub-groups.[5] Building on that information, one can compare the trait scores of the leader under examination who acts as policy entrepreneur with the scores of his or her peers to establish whether the leader exhibits a high, average, or low manifestation of a certain trait. Based on those classifications, it is possible to infer expectations regarding the instruments that a leader should be more or less likely to employ in his or her effort to implement foreign policy change in the domestic political arena.

In summary, the proposed leader-oriented theory of foreign policy change argues that acting upon their negative diagnosis of current policies, leaders act as change agents whose goal is to bring about major adjustments of their countries' foreign policy. The theory suggests that political beliefs are key with respect to the substantive adjustments that leaders seek to introduce, with the general tendencies of change pointing to either more cooperative or more conflictual policies. In turn, leadership traits are crucial concerning leaders' selection of policy entrepreneurial instruments and strategies that they employ to implement foreign policy change in the domestic political arena. Leaders can place greater emphasis on either group-oriented efforts or efforts that center around themselves.

Taken together, the preceding discussion leads to the following expectations concerning the role of leaders:

- *Triggering foreign policy change*: Leaders acting as change agents should publicly voice strong negative assessments of a current policy and call for fundamental revisions of that policy (expectation 1).
- *Guiding foreign policy change*: The political beliefs of leaders acting as change agents should systematically differ from the political beliefs of their predecessor (expectation 2a); and it should be possible to infer the direction in which leaders acting as change agents reorient their countries' foreign policy (that is, more cooperative or conflictual directions)

from the differences between their political beliefs and the beliefs of their predecessor (expectation 2b).
- *Implementing foreign policy change*: Leaders acting as change agents should engage in policy entrepreneurial activities when seeking to implement foreign policy change in the domestic political arena (expectation 3a); and leadership traits should indicate which entrepreneurial instruments and strategies leaders acting as change agents place particular emphasis on (expectation 3b).

Method and data

The leader-centered theory of foreign policy change seeks to explain episodes of major foreign policy change and conceptualizes leaders as key change agents in this regard. The remainder of this volume examines the internal validity and explanatory power of the proposed theory. To that end, it concentrates on an episode—in form of U.S. foreign policy toward Cuba under the Obama administration—that has been referred to in the literature as representing a major reorientation of policy. This set-up permits the examination of the proposed causal process of foreign policy change, which highlights the role of leaders as drivers of change.[6] Accordingly, this volume examines whether U.S. president Obama had a systematic, independent, and predictable effect on the outcome of interest, in form U.S. foreign policy change toward Cuba along the three stages of foreign policy change (that is, triggering change, guiding change, and implementing change) as proposed by the leader-centered theory of foreign policy change. The preceding sections have already provided information on the operationalizing of the different elements of the theory, for example, what constitutes a diagnosis of policy failure or how leaders' beliefs and traits are operationalized. The remainder of this section provides information on the methods and sources consulted to ascertain each element, with additional information on sources being provided in the empirical chapter (see Chapter Three of this volume).

The criteria set out by Hermann (1990) for the operationalization of problem/goal change and international orientation change respectively are used to ascertain whether the case under examination actually qualifies as an episode of major foreign policy change. As mentioned earlier, problem/goal change concerns alterations in instruments, commitment, and "expressed affect" which lead to "policy statements and policy actions incompatible with prior goal or problem stipulations." In turn, international orientation change "involves dramatic changes in both words and deeds in multiple issue areas with respect to the actor's relationship with external entities" (all quotes from Hermann 1990, 6). Changes in terms of rhetoric should become observable, for example, in statements of key decision makers or official documents issued by the government. Conversely, changes in terms of actions should become evident, for instance, by the formal conclusion of new partnerships (through declarations, treaties, and so on), joint diplomatic initiatives, the deepening of economic ties (for example, conclusion of free trade agreements), or activities in the field (for example, military activities such as exercises or even joint combat operations). This volume draws on governmental documents, media reports, and the scholarly literature to assess how fundamental a policy change has actually been.

The discussion pertaining to how a leader diagnoses existing policies ("triggering change") evolves around the three dimensions for evaluating the failure of a policy as set out in the public policy literature. To establish a leader's assessment of a policy along the programmatic, process, and political dimensions respectively, the volume draws primarily on original statements of the leader (speeches, interviews, autobiographies, and so on). In addition, the discussions incorporate assessments from the scholarly literature on how a leader evaluated certain policies. Finally, since negative evaluations of a policy by other political actors or society more broadly can lend additional impetus to the necessity of changing a policy, the discussion also draws on media reports, opinion polls, and the scholarly literature to ascertain whether such impetus or outright pressures existed as well.

For the other two dimensions of the theory (that is, "guiding change" and "implementing change"), congruence tests are employed to explore whether the expectations derived from the leader-centered theory fit with the empirical record (George and Bennett, 2005: Chapter 9). Thus, the discussion will first specify the expectations regarding the general direction of foreign policy change (cooperation or conflict) and the policy entrepreneurial instruments and strategies respectively. Those expectations are then tested against the empirical record to ascertain whether the theory's expectations are congruent with the real-world developments. To come up with the aforementioned expectations, automated content-analysis methods are employed to grasp a leader's political beliefs and traits respectively. The discussion now turns to how such leader profiles are generated.

The development of alternative policies ("guiding change") places leaders' political beliefs front and center. As outlined, this volume uses OCA to establish a leader's political beliefs. OCA belongs to the at-a-distance assessment techniques of leaders (Schafer, 2000; Post, 2005). Those techniques have been developed in response to the fact that researchers "rarely have direct access to a leader in a way that would allow for traditional psychological analysis" (Schafer, 2000: 512). To make up for this lack of direct and repeated access, at-a-distance techniques draw on leaders' verbal utterances to construct profiles which represent leaders' idiosyncratic characteristics in a systematic fashion.

To that end, OCA defines several qualitative and quantitative requirements for the sources based on which a profile is constructed. Importantly, as outlined, operational codes/political beliefs are considered domain-specific. Therefore, leaders' statements must relate to the specific issue area of foreign policy under examination rather than addressing other substantive areas of foreign policy, let alone non-foreign policy

Table 2.4: Source text requirements for Operational Code Analysis and Leadership Trait Analysis

Operational Code Analysis (OCA)	Leadership Trait Analysis (LTA)
Any verbal expression, including a complete speech, a press conference, or an interview	Spontaneous speech acts only
10+ speeches	100 speech acts (50 at the very least)
1500+ words per speech act or 15–20 coded verbs per speech act	150 words per speech act (100 at the very least)
Agnostic to audience/match to research question	Delivered in different contexts/in front of different audiences
Targeted toward policy issue under examination	Covering different issue areas
Targeted in case time/timing is of relevance for research question	Spanning a leader's tenure

Source: Adapted from Brummer et al (2020)

issues. The full list of OCA's expectations for source material is listed in Table 2.4.

Computer-based quantitative content analysis has become the standard in OCA research (Schafer and Walker, 2006b). Accordingly, the assembled source material is processed by employing the OCA coding scheme called "Verbs in Context System" (VICS) that is contained in the software platform "Profiler Plus" developed by *Social Science Automation*. The analysis, which as per the coding scheme's name zooms in on the verbs contained in the statements of leaders, yields index scores for each belief contained in OCA, with the scores ranging from either -1 to +1 or 0 to 1 (for details, see Walker et al, 1998; Schafer and Walker, 2006c, 2023).

In turn, differences between the OCA profiles of two leaders (here: between Obama and his predecessor George W. Bush) are established based on two-tailed t-tests with independent samples. It is those differences in leaders' beliefs that should guide the direction of changes in a country's foreign policy in more cooperative or more conflictual directions respectively. Expectations in this regard are inferred from the leaders' OCA profiles and subsequently tested against the empirical record. The latter discussions draw on governmental documents, media reports, and the scholarly literature to ascertain whether the expectations inferred from a leader's political beliefs, and differences therein compared to his or her predecessor, are indeed mirrored in the actual direction in which he or she has reoriented foreign policy.

The discussions pertaining to how leaders seek to bring about foreign policy change in the domestic political arena ("implementing change") zooms in on the instruments and strategies that leaders who act as policy entrepreneurs select in their efforts to implement policy change. However, rather than merely portraying what leaders have done in this regard, the leader-centered theory seeks to explain why leaders place greater emphasis on certain instruments and strategies than on others. To that end, the theory connects policy entrepreneurial actions with leaders' traits by suggesting that specific manifestations of leadership traits render the use of certain policy entrepreneurial instruments and strategies more or less likely. Leadership traits are identified by using another at-a-distance assessment technique of leaders, namely LTA.

LTA shares several similarities with OCA in terms of method (Hermann, 2005a, 2008). For instance, LTA profiles are nowadays also typically ascertained computer-based by using the "Profiler Plus" platform which, next to the OCA coding scheme, contains a coding scheme also for LTA. Further, LTA profiles are similarly based on leaders' verbal utterances. However, there are a few key differences between LTA and OCA. For instance, LTA scholarship typically assumes that leaders' traits are stable over time and across issue areas. This, together with the explicit preference for spontaneous statements, has implications for the compilation of source material. Accordingly, LTA profiles are constructed based on different sources than OCA profiles. The full list of LTA's expectations for source material is listed in Table 2.4.

The source material is processed using the aforementioned LTA coding scheme as contained in Profiler Plus. The analysis yields index scores for each of LTA's seven traits. For each trait, the score ranges from 0 to 1. More specifically, the dictionary-based coding scheme contains a set of words and expressions that indicate respectively high or low manifestations in a trait. The coding scheme identifies those words and expressions in the data (that is, leaders' statements) and calculates leaders' scores for each trait as the ratio of high and low expressions. For example, let us say the data contains 100 words and expressions that the coding scheme associates with TASK. Sixty of those words and expressions indicate high task focus (for example, achieve, efficiency, implementation, decisiveness) and 40 words and expressions indicate low task focus (for example, assistance, cohesion, loyalty, unity). This would lead to a leader's TASK score of .60.

In turn, whether a leader scores high, low, or average on a certain trait is established by comparing the scores with either the full "norming group" of world leaders or with a specific (regionally defined) sub-set of that norming group. Based on those classifications, it is possible to infer expectations regarding the preferences of leaders for certain policy entrepreneurial instruments and strategies over others, especially whether they lean more toward group-oriented instruments or instruments that put themselves front and center. It is those expectations that are subsequently tested against the empirical record. To that end, the discussions draw on multiple primary and secondary sources, including official governmental records, newspaper articles, and scholarly publications.

Conclusion

This chapter has developed a leader-centered theory of foreign policy change. While extant FPA literature acknowledges the role of leaders as possible drivers of foreign policy change, existing models render it next to impossible to ascertain any independent effect of leaders on said outcome. Thus, the leader-centered theory proposed in this volume seeks to ascertain the independent, systematic, and predictable effect of leaders on episodes of major foreign policy change in terms of both substance and process.

More specifically, the leader-centered theory conceptualizes foreign policy change as comprising three stages (see also Figure 2.1). The "triggering phase" suggests that leaders strongly and publicly criticize existing policies as patently failing or failed. Acting on such diagnosis, the "guiding phase" suggests that leaders reorient their countries' foreign policies in more cooperative or conflictual directions in accordance with their political beliefs. Finally, when seeking to bring about foreign policy change in the domestic political arena, the "implementing phase" argues that leaders select particular policy entrepreneurial instruments and strategies based on their leadership traits. Chapter Three will now apply this analytical framework to U.S. foreign policy toward Cuba during the Obama administration.

THREE

U.S. Foreign Policy Change toward Cuba under Obama

> Today, the United States of America is changing its relationship with the people of Cuba. In the most significant changes in our policy in more than fifty years, we will end an outdated approach that, for decades, has failed to advance our interests, and instead we will begin to normalize relations between our two countries.
>
> President Obama, Cuba Policy Détente Announcement, December 17, 2014[1]

In December 2014, U.S. president Barack Obama presented his ideas for a "Cuba policy détente." His underlying goal was "to cut loose the shackles of the past so as to reach for a better future" (Obama, 2014a). The president used the remainder of this second term to implement this policy. True, Obama's Cuba policy did share certain assumptions with the policies pursued by his predecessors, including emphasizing the necessity of both domestic reform in Cuba and reciprocity in terms of actions aimed at reducing tensions (LeoGrande and Kornbluh, 2014: 400). Having said that, Obama's "adventurous" (*The Economist*, 2016b) Cuba policy turned out to be fundamentally different from those of his predecessors. Indeed, terminating "one of the most misguided chapters in American foreign policy," Obama's "historic move" ushered in "sweeping changes to normalize relations with Cuba" and possibly even a "transformational era for millions of Cubans who have suffered as a result of more than 50 years of hostility between the two nations" (NYT, 2014a). LeoGrande (2020: 449) similarly refers to a "historic reversal" on par with Nixon's policy toward China.

This chapter opens with a discussion of whether U.S.–Cuba policy during the Obama administration actually qualifies as an instance of major policy change. It suggests that this is indeed the case as per Charles Hermann's typology. The chapter then explores whether President Obama had a systematic and predictable effect on the redirection of U.S. policy toward Cuba. To that end, following the "leader-centered theory of foreign policy change" with its three-step analytical framework introduced in Chapter Two of this volume, the chapter first examines whether Obama considered the Cuba policy of his predecessors as a major policy failure, which is considered as main trigger for the initiation of policy change ("triggering change"). The chapter then identifies Obama's political beliefs with respect to Cuba. Based on a comparison with the beliefs of his immediate predecessor George W. Bush, the chapter infers the direction of policy change that U.S. foreign policy should have taken based on Obama's "Cuba beliefs" and examines whether those expectations align with the empirical record ("guiding change"). Finally, the chapter ascertains Obama's leadership traits. On that basis, it develops expectations on how Obama should have gone about putting his goal of changing U.S.–Cuba policy into practice and finally matches those expectations with the empirical record ("implementing change").

An episode of major foreign policy change: U.S.–Cuba policy under the Obama administration

The first question is whether the Cuba policy of the Obama administration actually qualifies as an episode of major foreign policy change. Drawing on Hermann's typology, this volume considers both problem/goal change and international orientation change as instances of major policy change (Hermann, 1990). Empirically observable implications of such types of changes relate to both "words and deeds."

Hence, for the case under examination, one should expect major changes in terms of how the Obama administration perceived and described Cuba and its leadership in their statements and policy documents (that is, "words"). This should have been accompanied by and mirrored in significant adaptations regarding the instruments employed by the Obama administration toward Cuba spanning multiple areas of action, such as diplomacy, the economy, or the military (that is, "deeds"). Drawing on leaders' speeches, governmental documents, media reports, and the scholarly literature, the following discussion suggests that Obama administration's Cuba policy does indeed qualify as an example of major foreign policy change. To make this argument, the discussion first briefly describes key elements of the U.S.–Cuba policy that Obama "inherited" and then shows changes in "words" and "deeds" in said policy that were undertaken by the Obama administration (Table 3.1).

Core tenets of U.S.–Cuba policy

When Obama entered office in 2009, most of the core tenets of U.S.–Cuba policy had been in place since the early 1960s. Following the Cuban revolution under Fidel Castro, U.S. policy was first and foremost characterized by a hardline policy against the island which evolved around the imposition of diplomatic and economic sanctions. For example, in early 1961 President Eisenhower severed diplomatic relations with the country, which included the closing of the U.S. embassy in Havana. The following year, building on earlier restrictions, for example, on the export of sugar, the Kennedy administration imposed a comprehensive trade embargo (for example, Kaplowitz, 1998; Haney and Vanderbush, 2005; LeoGrande, 2015a; Haney, 2018).

Table 3.1: Key events in U.S.–Cuban relations during the Obama presidency

Date	Event
April 13, 2009	Easing of restrictions on travel and financial transactions (remittances) for family members
January 14, 2011	Easing of additional restrictions on travel and financial transactions (remittances)
November 6, 2012	Re-election of Barack Obama
June 2013	Secret back channel established involving figures close to Barack Obama and Raúl Castro
December 10, 2013	"Accidental" handshake between Barack Obama and Raúl Castro at the memorial service for Nelson Mandela in Johannesburg, South Africa
December 17, 2014	• Release from Cuban prison of USAID sub-contractor Alan Gross • Barack Obama's "Cuba policy détente" speech, which was complemented by a coordinated announcement by Raúl Castro
April 11, 2015	Meeting between Barack Obama and Raúl Castro at the 7th Summit of the Americas in Panama City, Panama
May 29, 2015	Removal of Cuba from state sponsors of terrorism list
July 20, 2015	Reopening of U.S. embassy in Havana (flag raising ceremony followed on August 14)
September 19, 2015	Easing of restrictions on travel, monetary transactions, and commerce
September 29, 2015	Meeting between Barack Obama and Raúl Castro at the United Nations General Assembly
March 20–22, 2016	Barack Obama conducts a state visit to Cuba
August 31, 2016	First scheduled commercial flight from the United States to Cuba in more than 50 years
September 27, 2016	Nomination of a U.S. ambassador to Cuba
October 14, 2016	Presidential Policy Directive on "United States-Cuba Normalization"
January 12, 2017	End of "wet foot, dry foot" policy

Subsequent decades by and large saw a continuation of this coercive policy, whose goals "evolved from regime change to punishment" (LeoGrande, 2015a: 943). Somewhat of an exception came in the 1970s under the administrations of Ford and Carter, the latter of whom agreed with Fidel Castro to set up "interest sections" in the respective capitals in 1977 and also lifted the travel ban. However, those more cooperative measures did not amount to the restoration of full diplomatic relations or the normalization of bilateral relations more generally. To the contrary, the relationship hardened again during the following years, as exemplified, for example, by the Reagan administration's decision to reinstate the travel ban and to add Cuba to the list of "state sponsors of terrorism."

After the end of the Cold War, restrictions were tightened even further, for example, through the adoption of the Cuban Democracy Act in 1992 and of the Cuban Liberty and Democratic Solidarity Act (commonly known as "Helms-Burton Act") in 1996. Importantly, the latter enshrined the embargo into law, which in turn meant that it could no longer be adjusted or outright terminated by a presidential decision (LeoGrande, 2015a: 947). However, based on the "Cuban Assets Control Regulations," the president was still in a position to introduce exceptions to the embargo. Finally, before Obama assumed the presidency, the George W. Bush administration further restricted sanctions in 2004. Measures to that effect included the imposition of even stricter limits on family visits to Cuba and on the flow of remittances (Sullivan, 2022: 1).

Key changes in U.S.–Cuba policy during the Obama administration

U.S.–Cuba policy changed noticeably from 2009 onward. Acting on the conviction "that engagement offers a path toward success where isolation has failed for more than 50 years" (White House, 2016c), the Obama administration ushered in a major redirection in U.S. policy toward Cuba. The underlying goal was to "normalize" the bilateral relationship with the country, as Obama had already promised on the presidential campaign trail (for example, AFP, 2008; Luo, 2008). In accordance with Hermann's definition of major foreign policy change, the fundamental redirection in U.S. foreign policy toward Cuba came in the form of both "words" and "deeds." The former (words) concerned a substantially different depiction of the bilateral relationship and its prospects. The latter (deeds) materialized in a host of concrete political decisions and actions that put the aforementioned changes in rhetoric into practice. Measures to that effect covered a variety of issue areas including diplomacy, security, economy, culture, and education.

On the level of "words," a notable change occurred with respect to the presentation of the bilateral relationship and its possible futures. True, just like previous administrations, the Obama administration also got out of its way to denounce the continued undemocratic nature of the Cuban regime and its detrimental consequences for the bilateral relationship. For example, Obama stated in 2011: "[W]e'll continue to seek ways to increase the independence of the Cuban people, who I believe are entitled to the same freedom and liberty as everyone else in this hemisphere" (Obama, 2011). The following year, at 6th Summit of the Americas held in Cartagena, Colombia, he justified Cuba's exclusion from the meeting by stating that "unlike the other countries that are participating, [Cuba] has not yet moved to democracy" (Calmes and Neumann, 2012).

Even after having initiated a major policy redirection toward Cuba, Obama repeatedly pointed out shortcomings of the country. For example, he argued that "we're still going to have serious issues with Cuba on not just the Cuban government's approach to its own people, but also regional issues and concerns" (Obama, 2015b); that "We continue to have differences with the Cuban government. We will continue to stand up for human rights" (White House, 2015d); or that "we cannot, and should not, ignore the very real differences that we have—about how we organize our governments, our economies, and our societies" (Obama, 2016e).

Yet at the same time, the Obama administration set itself apart from previous administrations by complementing its "traditional" critique of the Cuban regime with outlining a novel positive agenda for the bilateral relationship. This agenda placed particular emphasis on opportunities for collaboration and mutual benefits, for which in turn a different kind of engagement with the country was required (see next on the diagnosis of policy failure). To give but a few examples:

At the abovementioned 6th Summit of the Americas, Obama not only criticized Cuba's human rights record but also stated that:

> There may be an opportunity in the coming years as Cuba begins to look at where it needs to go in order to give its people the kind of prosperity and opportunity that it needs, that it starts loosening up some constraints within that country, and that's something that we will welcome. (AP, 2012c)

Then, in his landmark address on "Cuba policy détente" of December 2014, Obama emphasized joined interests and the potential of collaboration: "Where we can advance shared interests, we will." Accordingly, he pledged "to create more opportunities for the American and Cuban people, and begin a new chapter among the nations of the Americas" (Obama, 2014a).

The following year, at the 7th Summit of the Americas that was held in Panama City, Panama, in April 2015, Obama declared: "I think we are now in a position to move on a path toward the future, and leave behind some of the circumstances of the past that have made it so difficult, I think, for our countries to communicate" (White House, 2015b). Obama also stated that he and Castro had "agreed that we can continue to take steps forward that advance our mutual interests ... I'm optimistic that we'll continue to make progress and that this can indeed be a turning point—not just between the United States and Cuba, but for greater cooperation among countries across the region" (Obama, 2015b). Obama even expressly thanked Castro, with whom he held a joint press conference, "for the spirit of openness and courtesy that he has shown during our interactions" (White House, 2015b)—a statement that arguably few of Obama's predecessors would have made with regard to a Cuban president.

As a final example of the noticeable change in the portrayal of Cuba, Obama suggested in his "Address to the People of Cuba," which he delivered during a state visit to Cuba in Havana in March 2016, that "we … need to recognize how much we share. Because in many ways, the United States and Cuba are like two brothers who've been estranged for many years, even as we share the same blood" (Obama, 2016e). He similarly argued: "I'm also confident that Cuba can continue to play an important role in the hemisphere and around the globe—and my hope is, is that you can do so as a partner with the United States" (Obama, 2016e). The president concluded his speech with: "It is time, now, for us to leave the past behind. It is time for us to look forward to the future together … We can make this journey as friends, and as neighbors, and as family—together" (Obama, 2016e).

On the level of "deeds," those changes in the—now much more positive—rhetorical depiction of the bilateral relationship and its possible prospects in particular were mirrored in and implemented through a host of concrete decisions and actions. The following discussion serves to briefly highlight the breadth and depth of said change. Additional details on the actions and measures undertaken by the Obama administration are presented in the section on "implementing change" (see also Table 3.1).

The first measures were initiated in 2009 and 2011 respectively and concerned above all the easing of restrictions on travel and remittances to Cuba (White House, 2009a,

2011). Arguing that the promotion of human rights and democracy in Cuba serves U.S. interests, the administration decided in April 2009 to ease restrictions on family-related travel and on family-related remittances, among other things (White House, 2009a). This concerned both the frequency and duration of visits and the frequency and amount of money transfers (White House, 2009a). In 2011, those decisions were extended to include also non-family-related travel and non-family-related remittances, among other things (White House, 2011). Those measures showed that Obama "was willing to open the door toward greater engagement with Cuba—but at this point, only a crack" (Stolberg and Cave, 2009). Indeed, for the time being, additional steps toward the envisaged "normalization" of bilateral relations were hampered or even outright blocked by several factors, including continued resistance in the U.S. Congress also among Democrats. In addition, Obama had to seek re-election in 2012. His success in those elections, which included a strong performance among Cuban Americans, eased electoral considerations in his future dealings with Cuba (LeoGrande and Kornbluh, 2014: 397–8).

Another key obstacle came in the form of the continued imprisonment of an USAID sub-contractor, Alan Gross, in Cuba (Rhodes, 2019: 264), where he had been arrested in December 2009 and sentenced to 15 years in jail. After some 18 months of secret talks, Gross was eventually released in late 2014 in a prisoner swap, which also included the release of a U.S. agent from Cuba and of three Cuban agents who had been imprisoned in the United States (Obama, 2014a).[2] Indeed, it was by design that Obama gave his landmark "Cuban policy détente" speech on the very day, namely December 17, 2014, that Gross returned to the United States (Obama, 2014a). Obama's speech was complemented by a coordinated similar announcement by Cuban president Raúl Castro (*Guardian*, 2014),[3] with whom he had held a telephone conversation the previous day. That call represented "the first direct substantive contact between the leaders of the two countries in more than 50 years" (Baker, 2014).

Obama's policy détente speech ushered in multiple far-reaching adjustments in U.S.–Cuba policy (for details, see Laguardia Martinez et al, 2020: Chapter 5). For starters, Obama directly engaged with the Cuban president Raúl Castro. This included a three-day state visit to the country in March 2016. Another landmark change in the diplomatic realm concerned the restoration of full diplomatic relations with Cuba, which included the reopening of the U.S. embassy in Havana and the Cuban embassy in Washington, DC respectively in mid-2015. In the security realm, the administration decided to remove Cuba from the "state sponsors of terrorism" list, a decision which came into effect in late May 2015, and to start collaboration on questions such as port security and maritime navigation safety (White House, 2016c).

In terms of trade and travel, the Obama administration was not in a position to unilaterally remove the embargo that had been in place since the early 1960s. Having said that, the administration found several workarounds, particularly by making recourse to executive decisions, to mitigate the effects of the embargo (White House, 2016c). For example, further expanding the initial changes concerning travel and remittances as introduced in 2009 and 2011 respectively, the two countries agreed to set up direct flights (Sullivan, 2022). The first scheduled commercial flight from the United States to Cuba in more than 50 years, from Fort Lauderdale, Florida, to Santa Clara, took place on August 31, 2016 (Leiro, 2016). This was complemented by the authorization of private trips (as opposed to authorized educational tours), provided that those trips included "educational exchange activities that result in meaningful interaction with individuals in Cuba" (White House, 2016c). The administration also undertook efforts to deepen economic collaboration, for example, in the realms of telecommunication and agriculture.

Additional measures aimed at Cuban society more broadly. They entailed programs that allowed Cuban professionals to come to the United States as well as American students to go the Cuba. Also, the government provided (financial) incentives to deepen collaboration between universities. Cuban youth leaders and business entrepreneurs were also permitted to participate in high-profile programs and initiatives (for example, the Youth Leaders of the Americas Initiative), and measures in the realms of sports and culture were undertaken as well (White House, 2016c). Table 3.2 summarizes key changes in terms of "words" and "deeds" in U.S.–Cuba policy under the Obama administration.

Table 3.2: Examples of major changes in U.S.–Cuba policy under the Obama administration

Words	
	"Where we can advance shared interests, we will" (Barack Obama, Cuba policy détente speech, December 17, 2014)
	"I think we are now in a position to move on a path towards the future" (Barack Obama, joint press conference with Raúl Castro in Panama City, April 11, 2015)
	"We can make this journey as friends, and as neighbors, and as family—together" (Barack Obama, Address to the People of Cuba in Havana, March 22, 2016)
Deeds	
	Personal meetings between Barack Obama and Raúl Castro
	Restoration of full diplomatic relations incl. reopening of the U.S. embassy in Havana and the Cuban embassy in Washington, DC
	Loosening of travel restrictions
	Easing of financial transactions (remittances)
	Collaboration on cultural and educational issues

Note: For further details, see the section on "Implementing change: putting the Cuba policy détente into practice"

Triggering change: diagnosing a failing policy

The leader-centered theory of foreign policy change suggests that a leader's diagnosis of a policy failure is the key trigger for the reorientation of a policy. In turn, ascriptions of failure to a policy by other actors, for example, from within the administration, from his or her party, or from society more broadly (media, opinion polls, and so on), could reinforce the leader's own assessment concerning the need to change course. Following the public policy literature, a leader's diagnosis of a failed policy can potentially concern three dimensions. Such assessment could relate to: the inefficient use of resources or the overall ineffectiveness of existing policy in terms of goal-attainment (programmatic failure); deficiencies in the decision-making process through which existing policy emerged or limited support for existing policy by key constituencies (process failure); or negative representations and evaluations of existing policy in political discourse (political failure).

The ensuing expectation would be that Obama referred to the Cuba policy of his predecessor or predecessors as major failure along one or more of the three aforementioned dimensions of failure, and called for a fundamental revision of said policy accordingly. To ascertain whether this was the case, the following discussion draws on a variety of statements (speeches, interviews, and so on) by Obama that he made both prior to assuming office on the campaign trail and during his presidency in which he engaged with the U.S.–Cuba policy of past administrations. The aforementioned expectation is corroborated by the empirical evidence. Indeed, the following paragraphs illustrate Obama's unequivocally negative evaluation of U.S.–Cuba policy as conducted by his predecessors. He placed particular emphasis on the policy's "programmatic failure" in the sense that it failed to attain virtually any of its goals. The discussion also shows that Obama has been quite consistent in his diagnosis of failure, which pervaded his remarks made both during the election campaign and after assuming office.

Already during the presidential campaign, Obama left little doubt that he considered U.S. policy toward Cuba as utterly unsuccessful or, in his words, a "failure" (AFP, 2008) not least since it "has offered no clear vision for [the] future" (States News Service, 2008). On the campaign trail, he opined that "After eight years of the disastrous policies of George Bush ... [i]t's time for more than tough talk that never yields results. It's time for a new strategy" (States News Service, 2008). He similarly argued that it time for "trying new things" (Seelye and Falcone, 2007) and called "to shift policy" (AFP, 2008).

Importantly, Obama was of the opinion that existing policy not only failed to "advance[] our [U.S.] interests in the region" (States News Service, 2008) but was equally unsuccessful in improving the situation for ordinary Cubans. In one of his most stringent critiques of U.S.–Cuba policy, which he gave in May 2008 in front of the Cuban-American National Foundation, he stated:

> Throughout my entire life, there has been injustice in Cuba. Never, in my lifetime, have the people of Cuba known freedom. Never, in the lives of two generations of Cubans, have the people of Cuba known democracy. This is the terrible and tragic status quo that we have known for half a century—of elections that are anything but free or fair; of dissidents locked away in dark prison cells for the crime of speaking the truth. I won't stand for this injustice, you won't stand for this injustice, and together we will stand up for freedom in Cuba. (States News Service, 2008)

From this followed an obvious need for "offering a strategy for change" (States News Service, 2008).

For Obama, the key shortcomings of U.S. policy toward Cuba concerned the inefficient way in which it was conducted.

For example, he promised to reevaluate the key instruments hitherto employed by the United States to sanction Cuba, for example, in terms of restrictions on travel and the flow of remittances (AFP, 2008). However, Obama took particular exception with the refusal of U.S. presidents, including by the then-sitting President George W. Bush, to directly engage with the Cuban leadership. Accordingly, when prompted during a debate in July 2007 whether he would meet with leaders from authoritarian states without preconditions, Obama declared: "I would [be willing to meet without preconditions]. And the reason is this: that the notion that somehow not talking to countries is punishment to them, which has been the guiding diplomatic principle of this administration, is ridiculous" (Healy and Zeleny, 2007).

During the course of the campaign, Obama added certain qualifiers by stating that he would meet with the Cuban leader without preconditions provided that issues such as human rights and prisoner release and opening up the press would be discussed at such a meeting (AFP, 2008; Healy and Zeleny, 2008). For example, in a speech late May 2008 he stated: "My policy toward Cuba will be guided by one word: Libertad. And the road to freedom for all Cubans must begin with justice for Cuba's political prisoners, the rights of free speech, a free press and freedom of assembly; and it must lead to elections that are free and fair" (States News Service, 2008). Still, those caveats, which according to commentators "belie[d] the simple answer" (Rutenberg and Zeleny, 2008) that Obama had initially given to the question of whether or not to meet up with leaders like Castro, changed nothing in terms of Obama's general strongly negative assessment of U.S. policy toward Cuba.

After assuming office, Obama's analysis of the Cuba policy of his predecessors remained unchanged. On numerous occasions, he repeated his diagnosis of failure and the ensuing call for a fundamental redirection of policy. For example, at the 5th Summit of the Americas held in Port-of-Spain, Trinidad and Tobago, in April 2009, he criticized earlier U.S. behavior toward Cuba for "sticking to inflexible policies"—policies that in Obama's view "failed to advance liberty or opportunity for the Cuban people." Building on this assessment, Obama promised that

> The United States seeks a new beginning with Cuba ... I know that there's a longer journey that must be traveled to overcome to decades of mistrust, but there are critical steps we can take toward a new day ... I do believe that we can move U.S.–Cuban relations in a new direction. (White House, 2009b)

Similarly, in March 2011 during a trip to the Americas, Obama stated in Santiago, Chile, that "I will make this effort to try to break out of this history that's now lasted for longer than I've been alive" (Obama, 2011). The following year, he argued at the 6th Summit of the Americas held in Cartagena, Colombia: "I am not someone who brings to the table a lot of baggage from the past and I want to look at this problem in a new and different way" (AP, 2012b). And during a fundraiser in Miami, Florida, in November 2013, he stated that "the notion that the same policies that we put in place in 1961 would somehow still be as effective as they are today in the age of the Internet and Google and world travel doesn't make sense" (White House, 2013).

Obama also grounded his "Cuba policy détente" speech of December 2014, which represented the starting signal for "sweeping changes" (*The Economist*, 2014b), in an assessment of failed U.S. policy toward Cuba. In his speech, the president emphasized once again the blatant failure of U.S.–Cuba policy, which has been manifested by the fact that:

> [N]o other nation joins us in imposing these sanctions, and it has had little effect beyond providing the Cuban government with a rationale for restrictions on its people. Today, Cuba is still governed by the Castros and the

Communist Party that came to power half a century ago. Neither the American, nor Cuban people are well served by a rigid policy that is rooted in events that took place before most of us were born. (Obama, 2014a)

From this followed the by-then well-known implication in terms of ushering in fundamental changes in U.S. policy: "After all, these 50 years have shown that isolation has not worked. It's time for a new approach … I do not believe we can keep doing the same thing for over five decades and expect a different result" (Obama, 2014a). Accordingly, Obama pledged a "shift in policy towards Cuba" in form of "a policy of engagement [through which] we can more effectively stand up for our values and help the Cuban people help themselves as they move into the 21st century" (Obama, 2014a).

Also after his major policy détente announcement of late 2014, Obama continued to use his assessment of failure in U.S. policy toward Cuba to make the case for his proposed change of course. For example, just a few days after the policy détente speech, the president reiterated in his end of year press conference:

[W]hat I know deep in my bones is that if you've done the same thing for 50 years and nothing has changed, you should try something different if you want a different outcome. And this gives us an opportunity for a different outcome … I think it is not precedented for the President of the United States and the President of Cuba to make an announcement at the same time that they are moving towards normalizing relations. So there hasn't been anything like this in the past. (Obama, 2014b)

A few days later, he opined that "Cuba is a circumstance in which for 50 years, we have done the same thing over and over again and there hadn't been any change" (NPR, 2014). The president made similar statements, for example, in his 2015

State of the Union Address in January 2015 (White House, 2015a); in a joint press conference with Cuban president Raúl Castro at 7th Summit of the Americas in April 2015 (White House, 2015b); or in his speech before the United Nations General Assembly (UNGA) in September 2015 (White House, 2015d). A final example is Obama's Havana speech in March 2016 in which he argued that "What the United States was doing was not working. We have to have the courage to acknowledge that truth. A policy of isolation designed for the Cold War made little sense in the 21st century" (Obama, 2016e).

Assessments by other actors

While far from representing a consensus, as the discussion that follows shows, Obama was by no means alone in calling for a fundamental redirection of U.S. policy toward Cuba. Particular issue was taken with the comprehensive trade embargo. While it undoubtedly imposed huge financial costs on Cuba—estimates range to $117 billion (LeoGrande, 2015a: 955)—it was equally beyond doubt that it failed to accomplish its underlying goal of removing the Castro regime. Accordingly, scholars have criticized the U.S. sanctions regime against Cuba and the trade embargo in particular, suggesting that it "has never been effective at achieving its principal purpose: forcing Cuba's revolutionary regime out of power or bending it to Washington's will" (LeoGrande 2015a: 939) or that it has been an impediment to Cuba's democratization, not least through inhibiting pressure to this effect from third parties (Giuliano, 1998).

Similar assessments were voiced in leading left-leaning or liberal media. For example, on several occasions the *New York Times* questioned the effect of the embargo, which it considered "an utter failure" (NYT, 2014b), and called respectively for "a major policy shift" (NYT, 2014b) or "a new policy" toward Cuba (and Latin America more broadly) (NYT, 2008). In a similar vein, *The Economist* repeatedly denounced U.S.–Cuba policy, calling the embargo "wrongheaded and ineffective" (*The Economist*, 2008a) or "futile and counterproductive" (*The Economist*, 2009), and U.S.–Cuba policy a "demonstrable failure" (*The Economist*, 2008b) more broadly. It combined this critique with calls for a fundamental reversal of U.S. policy, opining that "It is high time to try a different approach" (*The Economist*, 2008b). Later, when more fundamental changes had still not been forthcoming, *The Economist* (2014a) postulated again that "the logic behind the embargo looks ever weaker" and that the Cuban regime "is buttressed, not undermined" by it. Last but not least, multiple opinion polls suggested that not only Americans in general but also Cuban Americans more specifically wanted to see adjustments in U.S. policy (for details, see Chapter Four of this volume). This included aspects such as the reestablishment of diplomatic relations, the easing of travel restrictions, and the lifting of the embargo (for example, Gallup, n.d.; FIU, 2008, 2011, 2014).

Having said that, Obama's suggestion to fundamentally change U.S. foreign policy toward Cuba was by no means unanimously appraised. Indeed, it proved to be highly contentious in the political realm.[4] Pushback not only came from the Republican side as might have been expected but also from within his own Democratic party. Obama's opponents took particular issue with his suggestion to, as one commentator put it, "stray[] from orthodoxy" (Rieff, 2008) by initiating a meeting with Cuba's leadership.

For example, the 2008 Republican presidential nominee John McCain opined that Obama "wants to sit down unconditionally for a presidential meeting with Raúl Castro. These steps would send the worst possible signal to Cuba's dictators—there is no need to undertake fundamental reforms, they can simply wait for a unilateral change in U.S. policy" (Luo, 2008). President Bush, whose policy was the immediate reference point for Obama's critique and his corresponding calls for change, also felt obliged to counter Obama's suggestions on changing course in U.S. policy toward Cuba specifically with respect to meeting up with the country's leader without preconditions: "What's lost by embracing a tyrant who puts his people in prison because of their political beliefs? What's lost is it will send the wrong message. It will send a discouraging message to those who wonder whether America will continue to work for the freedom of prisoners" (Stolberg, 2008).

On the side of the Democrats, Obama's proposal to meet up with rogue leaders like Castro similarly "touched off [a] firestorm" (AP, 2007), particularly among his rivals for the 2008 presidential nomination. Indeed, Hillary Rodham Clinton was just as outspoken in her critique of Obama's proposal as Republicans were, calling it "irresponsible and frankly naïve" (Seelye and Falcone, 2007). Akin to McCain's argument, Clinton also argued that she did not want "to see the power and prestige of the United States president put at risk by rushing into meetings" with Castro (Seelye and Falcone, 2007). Another of Obama's rivals for the Democratic presidential nomination, John Edwards, echoed that sentiment by similarly dwelling on the potential downsides for the United States that are likely to be associated with meeting up with rogue leaders (AP, 2007).

Hence, Obama did receive considerable critique for his initial ideas to alter course. Unsurprisingly, pushback did not end when he later further detailed and actually implemented the aspired change in policy, as the discussion on "Implementing Change" shows. Still, Obama was not to be deterred from his goal of shedding with a decade-old policy that in his view not only failed to realize but was actually detrimental to U.S. interests. The ensuing question concerns the direction in which this reorientation was supposed to occur, to which the discussion turns now.

Guiding change: toward a more cooperative U.S.–Cuba policy

The preceding section has shown that both before and after entering office Obama considered U.S.–Cuba policy as undertaken by his predecessors an unequivocal failure. The need to fundamentally reorient U.S.–Cuba policy followed logically from this diagnosis. In principle, two general directions for major adjustments were conceivable. On the one hand, Obama could have moved U.S. policy down an even more confrontational path, in terms of further tightening coercive measures toward Cuba in order to eventually topple the Castro regime. On the other hand, he could have reoriented U.S. policy into much more cooperative directions, in terms of seeking rapprochement through collaboration with the Cuban regime. Indeed, in and of itself Obama's above-cited diagnosis that decades worth of American Cuba policy failed to realize U.S. interests, thus needs to be overcome, could have suggested either avenue of action—and U.S. policy had seen fluctuations in one or the other direction in previous decades as well. Thus, the ensuing question concerns the direction in which American policy should have been redirected from the viewpoint of Obama.

To answer this question, this section applies the second part of the leader-oriented theory of foreign policy change to the case. Specifically, the following discussion first identifies Obama's operational codes (that is, political beliefs) with respect to Cuba and then compares them with those of Obama's predecessor, George W. Bush. According to the proposed framework, differences in the operational codes, thus political beliefs, between Obama and Bush should offer guidance in terms of the respectively more cooperative or more confrontational trajectory in which the former should have sought to reorient U.S.–Cuba policy during his presidency. The discussion shows that such differences do indeed exist. Hence, it is possible to infer expectations concerning the substantive direction of policy change under Obama, which point to a more cooperative American Cuba policy. It is those expectations that are subsequently compared with the empirical record to ascertain whether policy changes undertaken during the Obama administration were actually in accordance with

President Obama's political beliefs. The discussion suggests that expectations are indeed congruent with observed actions, which in turn lends support to the systematic and independent effect of the president on U.S.–Cuba policy and changes therein.

Obama and Bush: comparing their political beliefs on Cuba

Following OCA convention, the political beliefs of Presidents Bush and Obama have been ascertained based on their verbal statements on U.S. policy toward Cuba. The OCA literature suggests that typically at least 15,000 words (that is, ten speeches of at least 1,500 words each) should be analyzed to construct a profile. At the same time, the literature also shows that beliefs are domain-specific, thus sensitive to issue areas, which in turn means that a leader's belief on Cuba could be very different from, say, his beliefs on another Latin American country or the region as a whole. Against this background, the following profiles rest exclusively on statements that individually meet the 1,500 word or more criterion and jointly all focus on Cuba. Since no additional statements that met both criteria (length and substantive focus) could be identified, this means that at least for Bush the 15,000-word threshold was not fully met since, like in Obama's case, no additional extended statements on Cuba were found.

Specifically, for Bush a total of six speeches (totaling some 12,500 words) on Cuba were identified and analyzed. The speeches were drawn from georgewbush-whitehouse.archives.gov. In turn, for Obama four speeches (totaling some 16,000 words) on Cuba were analyzed. Speeches were drawn from obamawhitehouse.archives.gov and www.americanrhetoric.com. All speech acts were processed using the automated OCA coding scheme called "Verbs in Context System" (VICS) that runs on Profiler Plus (version 7.3.20).[5]

Figure 3.1 presents the results of the coding process. It shows that Obama's political beliefs are in part fundamentally

Figure 3.1: Comparison of the political beliefs of U.S. presidents Bush and Obama on Cuba

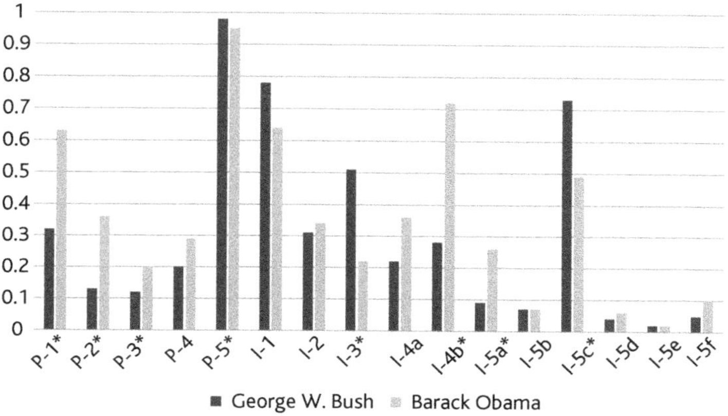

■ George W. Bush ■ Barack Obama

Note: Two-tailed t-tests (* significant at .05)

different from those of his predecessor. This concerns the selection of responses and instruments as indicated by the instrumental beliefs and even more so the diagnosis of the situation as shown in the scores for the philosophical beliefs. Indeed, Obama exhibits a markedly more positive view of the political environment with regard to Cuba than Bush (P-1), which indicates the perception of a much more friendly, trustworthy, and benign context. Similarly, Obama is more optimistic than Bush to accomplish his political goals with respect to Cuba (P-2). Relatedly, Obama's scores point to a greater belief in the predictability of future developments (P-3) and a corresponding smaller role of chance (P-5). In terms of instrumental beliefs, the scores suggest that Obama is less willing to take risks in his policies toward Cuba than Bush (I-3). At the same time, they point to greater flexibility on part of Obama when selecting policy instruments (I-4b), where he specifically places less emphasis on appeals and more emphasis on rewards than Bush (I-5).

Taken together, the differences in the "Cuba beliefs" of Obama compared to those of his predecessor suggest that he should have pursued a systematically different policy toward Cuba. Indeed, the diagnosis of a considerably more benign political context in particular suggests that Obama should have engaged in a notably more cooperative approach toward Cuba compared to Bush. So rather than further tightening U.S. policy toward Cuba, thereby further extending Bush's measures, Obama's beliefs suggest that he should have been willing to explore opportunities for collaboration in his Cuba policy. While the scores do not specifically indicate who the envisaged partner or partners for such cooperation should be, the latter could possibly include the Cuban leadership.

Further, when steering a new course, Obama should have been rather confident in his ability to realize his goals. In terms of ends-means relationships, the scores suggest that Obama should have been hesitant to take risks in his policies toward Cuba. Finally, he should have shown considerable flexibility in terms of selecting policy instruments toward Cuba, with placing a new and explicit emphasis on offering rewards to the Cuban addressees of his policy.

Changes in U.S.–Cuba policy under Obama

The aforementioned expectations are corroborated by the empirical record. As already briefly outlined in the section on "an episode of major policy change" and with a much more extensive discussion to follow in the section on "implementing change," suffice it to say at this point that Obama did indeed engage in a significantly more cooperative behavior toward Cuba. This verdict is not only true compared to his immediate predecessor George W. Bush but, following his "Cuba policy détente" announcement of late 2014, to all U.S. presidents since the break-up of bilateral relations in the early 1960s. Key landmarks of Obama's policy of "normalization" and the ensuing rapprochement between the United States and

Cuba included: highly symbolic meetings between him and President Castro including a state visit to Cuba; the reopening of embassies; the removal of Cuba from the state sponsors of terrorism list; the easing of travel restrictions and financial transactions; and the resumption of direct flights, among other things.

The only expectation that at first glance does not seem to be matched by the empirical record is that Obama should have been reluctant to take risks. Indeed, there was virtually not a single decision of at least some import in the rollout of his normalization policy toward Cuba that was not met with harsh criticism. As had been the case when Obama had initially voiced his ideas of substantially altering U.S.–Cuba policy during the 2008 presidential campaign, pushback was not confined to the Republican side but also came from Obama's own party, as will be detailed in the following section. Hence, changing course in U.S.–Cuba policy definitely entailed significant political risk.

At the same time, Obama undertook virtually all of the far-reaching changes in U.S.–Cuba policy only after his re-election to a second (and final) presidential term. This is by no means to say that those actions were therefore free of political risk since they could have, for example, diminished the president's standing and political capital, which in turn could have cost him in other areas of policy making. At the same time, any changes in Cuba policy introduced in the second term did no longer jeopardize Obama's personal future electoral prospects. In this sense, Obama himself suggested that "it's easier for a president to do [moves like the Cuba diplomatic initiative] at the end of this term than a new president coming in" (NPR, 2014).

Overall, then, there is considerable congruence between Obama's "Cuba beliefs" on the one hand and the direction in which U.S.–Cuba policy was actually reoriented during his administration. This suggests that Obama's beliefs could have been crucial in guiding the actions of his administration toward Cuba, as proposed by the theoretical model. Yet was it really beliefs that drove his policies or was it rather much more instrumental calculations grounded in the need to win elections that made Obama redirect U.S.–Cuba policy?

Undoubtedly, pursuing a much more cooperative Cuba policy than his predecessors contained the promise of electoral benefits. As mentioned, such policy changes were increasingly favored by a majority of the U.S. population. Importantly, support for reorienting U.S.–Cuba policy was not confined to adherents of the Democrats but also included Republican supporters, including typically Republican-leaning Cuban Americans in the swing state of Florida (for example, FIU, 2008, 2011, 2014). As LeoGrande and Kornbluh (2014: 368) suggest, "Obama aimed to win over moderates—a growing segment of the [Cuban American] community according to opinion polls." From this vantage point, changing policy into more cooperative directions seemed like prudent politics, and successful politics on top: Obama won Florida in both the 2008 and the 2012 presidential elections. Hence, it would surely be questionable to dismiss electoral considerations out of hand. Indeed, Obama's "outreach to Cuba may partly [have been] a way of repaying young Hispanic Democrats who helped him bring to power" (*The Economist*, 2015).

At the same time, two issues in particular suggest that Obama was driven by more than just electoral concerns. The first relates to the persistency with which he pursued the policy of normalizing relations with Cuba for a decade, if not longer. According to Luo (2008) Obama had already voiced the idea of "normalizing" relations with Cuba during a campaign for the U.S. Senate in 2003. The second issue relates to the specific timing of Obama's actions. As shown in greater detail next, the main push toward fundamentally redirecting U.S.–Cuba policy came after his re-election for a second (and final) term. Hence, had it only been for electoral concerns, Obama could have simply ended his efforts to reverse policy after 2012, leaving it with the initial, and still quite modest, reforms (for example, concerning travel and financial transactions) that had been introduced in 2009 and 2011 respectively. Yet it was in his second term that Obama announced and implemented the "Cuba policy détente" in earnest. This, in turn, suggests that substantive considerations and goals played a key role in guiding his actions. Thus, the argument would be that while electoral considerations were by no means irrelevant, it was first and foremost conviction that drove Obama's policy to fundamentally redirect U.S. policy toward Cuba. Or, in Obama's own words: "I believe that the best way to advance American interests and values, and the best way to help the Cuban people improve their lives, is through engagement" (Obama, 2016a). The following section shows how Obama sought to put into practice this policy of engagement.

Implementing change: putting the Cuba policy détente into practice

So far, the discussion has outlined the perceived need of policy change based on a diagnosis of failure of existing policies on the part of Obama as well as the substantive direction in which said policy change should have unfolded based on Obama's reading and understanding of the policy area. The remaining question is how the president tried to bring about the aspired redirection in U.S.–Cuba policy. Indeed, calling for policy change is one thing; delivering on such promises is another, as Obama himself had already noted on the campaign trail: "I know what the easy thing is to do for American politicians. Every four years, they come down to Miami, they talk tough, they go back to Washington and nothing changes in Cuba" (Zeleny, 2008).

Hence, the question is how Obama did go about putting into practice the proposed changes in U.S. policy toward Cuba. Accordingly, the focus of the discussion shifts to the instruments that Obama employed when acting as policy entrepreneur in the domestic political arena. The leader-centered theory proposed in this book considers the selection of political entrepreneurial instruments as a function of a leader's personality traits. Against this background, this section first identifies Obama's leadership traits, then develops expectations based on those traits in terms of which policy entrepreneurial instruments he was particularly likely to employ, and finally tests those expectations against the empirical record.

Obama's leadership traits

As per LTA convention, Obama's leadership traits are identified based exclusively on spontaneous statements of his. Following from the assumption that leaders exhibit a specific manifestation of traits across issue areas, statements concern not only Cuba policy but also foreign relations more broadly as well as domestic political issues. A total of 100 spontaneous statements of at least (and often times many more than) 100 words in length from throughout Obama's tenure in office (2009–2017) were randomly selected. The statements were drawn from www.americanrhetoric.com, obamawhitehouse. archives.gov, www.npr.org, and bbc.com. The spontaneous speech acts (totaling some 43,000 words) were processed using the automated LTA coding scheme that runs on Profiler Plus (version 7.3.20).[6]

Table 3.3 depicts the results of the coding process. To put Obama's leadership trait scores into perspective, the table also shows the mean scores of LTA's "Anglo-American" norming group. The comparison suggests that Obama has a considerably higher level of self-confidence (SC) than the norming group leaders (two standard deviations above the mean). In addition, Obama scores high—that is, one standard deviation above the mean—in three other traits, namely belief in the ability to control events (BACE), need for power (PWR), and conceptual complexity (CC). Conversely, Obama's scores are average on the remaining three traits covered in LTA, namely task focus (TASK), distrust of others (DIS), and in-group bias (IGB).

Table 3.3: Obama's leadership traits

Decision makers Trait	Obama	Anglo-American norming group (n=15)	Z scores	Obama *compared* to Anglo-American norming group	Expectation for policy entrepreneurial action
Belief in the ability to control events (BACE)	.40	.36 (.04)	1.0	High	Engage in leading by example
Self-confidence (SC)	.61	.45 (.08)	2.0	Very high	
Conceptual complexity (CC)	.65	.60 (.05)	1.0	High	Engage in scaling up advocacy efforts
Need for power (PWR)	.28	.24 (.04)	1.0	High	Engage in transforming institutions
Task focus (TASK)	.64	.62 (.06)	0.5	Average	n/a
Distrust of others (DIS)	.13	.12 (.03)	0.33	Average	n/a
In-group bias (IGB)	.14	.13 (.03)	0.33	Average	n/a

Note: Z scores based on comparison of Obama's scores with Anglo-American norming group. Standard deviations in parenthesis.

Linking traits and policy entrepreneurial instruments

The preceding LTA profile suggests that Obama had high or very high manifestations in four leadership traits, pertaining to BACE, PWR, CC and SC. The ensuing question is what those trait scores suggest in terms of the use of specific policy entrepreneurial instruments. The expectations put forward by the leader-centered theory of foreign policy change suggests the following:

The relatively strong BACE and even more so the extremely high level of SC should have rendered the use of "leading by example" by Obama particularly likely. Further, the relatively high level of CC suggests that Obama should have been predisposed to engage in "scaling up advocacy efforts" to bring about policy change. Last, the relatively high PWR should have rendered more likely the "transformation of institutions" in order to realize the aspired policy change. Conversely, the average manifestations in terms of TASK, DIS and IGB do not allow clear predictions in terms of "team building." This is also why the following discussion focuses on the three policy entrepreneurial instruments—in the form of leading by example, scaling up advocacy efforts, and transforming institutions—for which theoretical expectations could be developed.

Obama as policy entrepreneur

The previous examination of President Obama's leadership traits suggests that he should have been particularly likely to engage in three types of policy entrepreneurial actions: leading by example, scaling up advocacy efforts, and transforming institutions. The following discussions show that Obama did indeed make extensive use of policy entrepreneurial instruments. His actions confirm the aforementioned expectations in that he led by example, scaled up advocacy

U.S. FOREIGN POLICY CHANGE TOWARD CUBA UNDER OBAMA

Table 3.4: Obama's use of policy entrepreneurial instruments

Policy entrepreneurial instrument	Usage
Leading by example	Numerous activities pertaining to verbal declarations, physical actions, and political decisions that introduced new ideas and measures or terminated established policies respectively.
Scaling up advocacy efforts	Significant increase in scope of measures over time (2009 to 2014), followed by additional measures to maintain momentum for change (2015 to 2017).
Transforming institutions	Sustained but ultimately unsuccessful efforts to win over Congress for his policy of rapprochement.

efforts, and, albeit largely unsuccessfully, sought to transform institutions (Table 3.4).

To illustrate those findings, the following discussion expands on and deepens the earlier outlines of policy changes that the Obama administration ushered in especially after the 2014 declaration of a "Cuban policy détente" (see also Table 3.1). Those changes were so deep-running that they ultimately "left in place only a shell of the decades-old policy" (Haney, 2018: 176) that the president had inherited when assuming office in 2009.

Leading by example

Leading by example means that decision makers "tak[e] an idea and turn[] it into action themselves" (Mintrom, 2020: 19) through verbal declarations or physical actions, or both. This can be done, for example, by making far-reaching proclamations in which they chart new directions of policy or by engaging in symbolic actions for instance in the form of gestures or visits. They can similarly make a point by not doing something, for example, by refraining from repeating previously voiced positions or by terminating certain measures. Evaluated against this definition, there is no doubt that Obama did lead by example. He did so both rhetorically by making landmark statements and physically by engaging in activities and promoting policy decisions that clearly broke with at times decades-old U.S. policy.

Changes in rhetoric have already been outlined in the section on "An episode of major foreign policy change." Multiple examples given there showed that Obama offered a decidedly different depiction of the bilateral relationship, and its prospects in particular, with the aim being that "the United States begins a new chapter in our relationship with Cuba" (Obama, 2015a). Obama's verbal advocacy of a policy of engagement and an ensuing normalization in bilateral relations thus represented a clear break with the past, suggesting that the president personally paved the way for fundamental changes in U.S.–Cuba policy on this rhetorical level.

In turn, the following paragraphs focus on the level of actions. They provide details on specific activities undertaken and measures introduced by Obama and his administration through which the president exerted leadership in terms of opening up the aspired "new chapter" in U.S.–Cuba relations. The discussions first zoom in on what have arguably been the most symbolic examples of Obama's efforts to lead by example, in the form of his encounters with his Cuban counterpart Raúl Castro. This is followed by a discussion on additional measures such as the reopening of embassies that similarly illustrate the extent to which a fundamental shift from the policy of previous governments occurred under Obama's lead.

Obama lived up to his campaign promise to meet his Cuban counterpart, thereby taking a symbolic personal lead in the proposed policy of engagement. A first, albeit unplanned encounter came in Johannesburg, South Africa, in December 2013 on the occasion of a memorial service for former South African president Nelson Mandela where the two leaders shook hands and exchanged a few words. The gesture was notable since—following Bill Clinton and Fidel Castro at the UN Millennium Summit in New York in 2000—it was the just the second time since the break-up of diplomatic relations in the early 1960s that leaders from the two countries greeted each other (AFP, 2013a). At the same time, the White House went out of its way to emphasize that the meeting was not "pre-planned" (AFP, 2013b) in advance and also did not usher in a fundamental change in U.S. policy. Still, certain hopes were read into the handshake, which according to a commentator "can also mark the beginning of a thawing of relations" (Shear, 2013). Even a Cuban government website stated: "[M]ay this image [of the meeting of the two leaders] be the beginning of the end of the US aggression against Cuba" (AFP, 2013a).

The next meeting between Obama and Castro was pre-planned. It occurred during the 7th Summit of the Americas that was held in Panama City, Panama, in April 2015 and brought together the heads of states and governments of the member states of the Organization of American States (OAS). Although a meeting with Castro was not listed on Obama's official agenda, the president traveled to Panama City with the clear expectation of meeting up with his Cuban counterpart (Hirschfeld Davis and Archibold, 2015a). The meeting, which had been prepared by a phone call between Obama and Castro and an exchange between the two countries' foreign ministers (Hirschfeld Davis and Archibold, 2015b), did eventually take place. It lasted for about an hour and was preceded by a joint press conference of the two presidents (White House, 2015b). The meeting was notable not only since it was the first such encounter between the presidents of the two countries in some 50 years. It was equally notable due to the fact that Cuba had been permitted to participate in the summit meeting in the first place.

Indeed, it was upon the insistence of the United States that Cuba had been expelled from the OAS in 1962. Accordingly, it could not participate in OAS gatherings including the summit meetings. This was true also for the two summits that had been staged earlier in Obama's tenure, in Port-of-Spain, Trinidad and Tobago, in 2009 and Cartagena, Colombia, in 2012 respectively. On both occasions, Obama faced strong criticism for upholding his predecessors' refusal to allow Cuba to attend those summits. For example, at the 2012 meeting "Leftist Latin American leaders repeatedly harangued the United States for continuing to insist that the communist run nation be barred from the 18-year-old Summit of the Americas circuit" (AP, 2012b).[7] Three leftist countries including Venezuela even threatened to boycott the next summit should Cuba still be prohibited to attend (AP, 2012b).

Indeed, bar receiving back-up from the conservative Canadian Prime Minister Stephen Harper, the 2012 summit showed how little support there was in the Americas for the U.S. policy of isolating Cuba. As discussed before, the essentially isolated position of the United States played a key role in Obama's diagnosis of a fundamentally flawed U.S. policy toward Cuba. At the same time, Obama himself refrained from supporting, thus blocked, a declaration at the 2012 summit that would have called for the inclusion of Cuba at the next summit meeting—a move through which the president sought to "avoid[] antagonizing some Cuban-American voters in Florida, a crucial battleground state in this year's presidential election" (Calmes and Neuman, 2012). Then, three years later, Obama expressly welcomed Cuba's participation (Obama, 2015a). In addition, he deliberately used the 2015 summit to "reaffirm" (Obama, 2015b) the fundamental change in U.S.–Cuba policy that he had announced just a few months earlier in his "Cuba policy détente" declaration by meeting up with Castro.

The next meeting between Obama and Castro occurred on the occasion of the United Nations General Assembly (UNGA) in New York in late September 2015.[8] The meeting—which "not too many years ago … would have been utterly unthinkable" (CNN, 2015)—was held just a few days after Obama had lived up to his policy détente speech by putting into practice concrete measures to ease restrictions on travel, monetary transactions, and commerce. On that occasion, Obama had also had a phone conversation with Castro in which they explored measures to advance cooperation between their countries (Hirschfeld Davis, 2015b). The question of further advancing the normalization of bilateral relations then also dominated the personal exchange between the two presidents on the sidelines of the UNGA (Harris, 2015).

While commentators referred to the UNGA meeting as "capp[ing] a period of remarkable change" (Harris, 2015), the most high-profile meeting was still about to come. It occurred in mid-March 2016 when Obama paid a state visit to Cuba. The president was accompanied by cabinet members, some 40 members of Congress from both sides of the aisle,[9] which was the "largest such delegation" during Obama's presidency (Obama, 2016d), business leaders, and the First Family, among others. It was the first visit to Cuba by a sitting U.S. president since Calvin Coolidge's in 1928 and was lauded as representing "a symbolic culmination of a process of rapprochement" (*The Economist*, 2016a) between the two countries. The visit, which came shortly after the introduction of additional steps by the administration to ease travel restrictions for U.S. citizens to Cuba (now permitting also educational travel) as well as an announcement on port security, included:

- a U.S. embassy "meet and greet" event on March 20 in which Obama thanked the staff for their contributions to rolling out the process of normalizing relations with Cuba (Obama, 2016b);

- a bilateral meeting with President Castro at the Revolutionary Palace on March 21 in which both further steps in the normalization process and contentious issues such as human rights were discussed, followed by an almost hour-long joint press conference (Obama, 2016d) where "The apparent rapport between the two presidents ... was a striking display of warmth" (Hirschfeld Davis and Cave, 2016);[10]
- an exchange with Cuban entrepreneurs the same day where business opportunities and prospects were discussed and the inclusion of Cuban entrepreneurs in the Young Leaders in the Americas Initiative and the Global Entrepreneurship Summit respectively was announced (Obama, 2016c);
- a direct engagement with the Cuban people through a speech at the Grand Theater of Havana on March 22 which was broadcast live in Cuba and also attended by President Castro (Obama, 2016e); and
- a meeting with members of civil society, including critics of the regime,[11] at the U.S. embassy following Obama's speech (for details on the visit, see Rhodes, 2019: 352–9).[12]

Obama went out of his way to emphasize the importance that he ascribed to the visit. For example, he stated that "it's a historic opportunity to engage directly with the Cuban people and to forge new agreements and commercial deals, to build new ties between our two peoples, and for me to lay out my vision for a future that's brighter than our past" (Obama, 2016b). He similarly re-emphasized that normalization was a process that will not be completed overnight but will take time to unfold and will also encounter challenges along the way. He argued that "We agree that a long and complex path still lies ahead" (Hirschfeld Davis and Cave, 2016), not least since additional political and economic reforms on the part of the Cuban regime would be required as would be the lifting of the U.S. embargo against Cuba (for example, Obama, 2016c, 2016d). Consequently, rather than representing the "culmination" of his efforts to normalize U.S.–Cuban relations as commentators had suggested, for Obama the visit was but another milestone in the process of "setting a new chapter in Cuban American relations" (Obama, 2016d).

Yet Obama not only led the way by engaging in actions that his predecessors shied away from. He also fundamentally redirected the course of U.S.–Cuba policy by easing or outright terminating the decisions of previous administrations. Examples include reversals in the policies regulating travel to and financial transactions (esp. remittances) with Cuba or, as already referred to, with respect to blocking the country's participation in OAS meetings. The following paragraphs discuss two additional areas of action where such reversals of what until then had been core tenets of U.S.–Cuba policy happened, in the form of the removal of Cuba from the state sponsors of terrorism list and the reopening of embassies.

Cuba had been placed on the state sponsors of terrorism list by the Reagan administration in 1982. As promised by Obama in his "Cuba policy détente" speech of December 2014, the country was eventually removed from the list in late May 2015. Obama went out of his way to explain that this decision must not be seen as offering blanket support to Cuba's non-democratic regime but that it was merely to acknowledge in a much more confined substantive sense that Cuba had no longer supported terrorist groups in recent months. Obama noted accordingly: "The criteria is very straightforward. Is this particular country considered a state sponsor of terrorism—not, do we agree with them on everything, not whether they engage in repressive or authoritarian activities in their own country" (Hirschfeld Davis, 2015a). Obama acted on this by sending a report to Congress in mid-April 2014 which certified that Cuba had not been a sponsor of terrorism during the previous six months (White House, 2015c). Congress could have blocked the decision through a joint resolution but did not do so. As result, after a 45-day notification period the decision entered into force on May 29, 2015. However, since the trade embargo remained in place, the practical effects of this delisting remained limited (LeoGrande, 2015a: 952).

Another example is the reopening of the U.S. embassy in Havana, along with the Cuban embassy in Washington, DC. LeoGrande (2015b: 485) even refers to this decision as the "[b]y far ... most important change" introduced by Obama "because of its symbolism." Diplomatic relations between the two countries had been broken off in 1961. In 1977, "interest sections" were set up in Washington, DC and Havana respectively as quasi-representations of the countries on the other's territory. In his Cuba policy détente speech, Obama pledged to change this by re-establishing the U.S. embassy in Havana (Obama, 2014a). The decision was formally announced by the president on July 1, 2015. The embassy was re-opened on July 20, 2015, and the official flag raising ceremony in Havana was held in the presence of U.S. Foreign Secretary John Kerry—who was the first American foreign secretary to visit Cuba in 70 years (Laguardia Martinez et al, 2020: 64)—on August 14, 2015 (U.S. Department of State, 2015). Obama was optimistic about the positive effects that this particular reversal of U.S.–Cuba policy would entail: "We're confident that it [the reopening of the U.S. embassy] can lead to an improved dialogue. And our bottom line at the end is, is that it can lead to an improved set of prospects for the Cuban people" (Obama, 2015b).

Then, in late September 2016 Obama nominated Jeffrey DeLaurentis for the post of ambassador. Following two earlier postings in Cuba, DeLaurentis had already led the U.S. Interest Section in Havana since mid-2014 and then served as acting U.S. ambassador to Cuba since mid-2015. He was thus a well-established figure in U.S.–Cuban relations whose appointment would have meant another key step in the normalization of bilateral relations (White House, 2016e). Indeed, DeLaurentis would have been the first U.S. ambassador to Cuba in some 55 years. However, the U.S. Senate never ratified the nomination, which in turn meant that DeLaurentis maintained his acting (*ad interim*) status until his departure from Cuba in mid-2017. Conversely, the Cuban ambassador to the United States, José Ramón Cabañas Rodríguez, had been accredited already in September 2015.

Overall, then, Obama did engage in numerous activities pertaining to verbal declarations, physical actions, and political decisions that qualify as instances of leading by example. In terms of rhetoric, he offered a very different depiction of the relationship, and opportunities therein, with Cuba. He also followed up his promise to meet up with the Cuban leadership, which included a highly symbolic state visit to Cuba. Last but by no means least, Obama and his administration made a point by reversing or terminating long-held positions and policies, as exemplified by the reopening of an embassy in Havana and Cuba's removal from the state sponsors of terrorism list.

Scaling up advocacy efforts

Obama's leadership traits also suggest that a scaling-up of advocacy efforts and ensuing actions should have been discernable. This policy entrepreneurial instrument emphasizes the importance of sequencing and timing of action in ushering in policy change. The assumption is that rather than introducing sweeping changes in one motion (which often times tends to politically impossible), leaders trigger processes of change with a few initial and, in terms of substance and scope, not necessarily far-reaching decisions. Importantly, those initial decisions represent the building blocks from which additional and more far-reaching reforms are subsequently introduced.

This expectation of Obama essentially starting "slow" with some modest reforms that over time are significantly expanded in terms of substance and scope is supported by the empirical evidence. Indeed, Obama "merely" introduced a few initial reforms in U.S.–Cuba policy during his first few years in office, particularly with respect to the easing of travel restrictions and remittances, both of which had been tightened just a few years earlier under Obama's predecessor George W. Bush. Commentators referred to those early decisions as "the most significant shift in United States policy toward Cuba in decades, and it is a reversal of the hard line taken by former President George W. Bush" (Stolberg and Cave, 2009).[13] Obama himself similarly depicted those changes as breaking new grounds: "Since taking office, I've announced the most significant changes to my nation's policy towards Cuba in decades" (Obama, 2011).

However, those initial changes were quite modest overall, leaving U.S.–Cuba policy similar to (for example, Prevost, 2011; Laguardia Martinez et al, 2020: Chapter 4) and, on balance, arguably also "still more restrictive" (LeoGrande and Kornbluh, 2014: 372) than it had been during the Carter and Clinton administrations respectively. LeoGrande and Kornbluh (2014: 401) therefore wondered in mid-2014 whether "Obama could summon the courage to cut it during his second-term," in the sense of "trying something truly new." Developments that unfolded afterwards suggest that the answer to this question is affirmative. Indeed, in his second term Obama "risked a policy change toward Cuba" (Laguardia Martinez et al, 2020: 54) which ushered in fundamental changes.

To keep up momentum for reform, the Obama administration engaged in back-channel exchanges with Cuba to engage the country over issues such as migration, drug trafficking, and the postal service (for example, U.S. Department of State, 2010; LeoGrande and Kornbluh, 2014: Chapter 9). Then, in mid-2013, an additional secret back channel was opened with the facilitation and support of Pope Francis and the Canadian government.[14] This time, the exchanges involved people close to President Obama (in form of Deputy National Security Advisor for Strategic Communications, Ben Rhodes) and President Castro (in form his son Alejandro) respectively (for details, see Rhodes, 2019: 209–17, 262–6, 283–9, 300–4; also Kornbluh and LeoGrande, 2019). Those talks eventually led to much more far-reaching reforms, which Obama announced in his "Cuban policy détente" speech of December 2014. This announcement as such, which promised a host of fundamental changes in U.S.–Cuba policy (reopening of embassies, further easing of travel restrictions, and so on), represented the most ambitious and visible element of Obama's upscaling of his advocacy effort to reorient U.S. policy.

The rollout of the proposed measures was first and foremost handled behind the scenes by bureaucratic actors from multiple departments. A key role in this context played the so-called "Bilateral Commission" which was set up in September 2015 for the purpose of putting normalization into practice. Yet Obama made sure that the change process was not relegated to the political sidelines or fell off the cliff altogether. He did so by engaging in several high-profile measures to keep up the momentum for change.

As shown before, those measures included the bilateral meeting with Castro at the 7th Summit of the Americas in Panama City, Panama, in 2015 and his state visit to Cuba the following year. With regard to the latter, Obama explicitly stated that it offered "an opportunity to keep moving forward" (Obama, 2016a). Indeed, Obama deliberately used his 2016 state visit to Cuba to make another major push to usher in as much change as possible during the remaining months of his presidency. In this sense, Deputy National Security Advisor Rhodes stated with respect to the timing of Obama's visit "that, in fact, going earlier this year would allow us to try to get more done, both around his visit and in the days and months that follow … So our objective here is to do as much as we can with the time we have remaining to make this an irreversible policy" (White House, 2016b). LeoGrande (2016a: 26) echoes this assessment by stating that with his visit Obama "sought to accelerate the pace of normalization during his last ten months in office."

Also after his visit to Cuba, Obama and his administration tried to keep up the momentum of his policy of normalization. This not only came in the form of multiple specific policy decisions taken on the administrative level (see Laguardia Martinez et al, 2020: Chapter 5) but also included high-profile measures that were aimed at maintaining political momentum for the process of change. One was the nomination of Jeffrey DeLaurentis for the post of U.S. ambassador to Cuba in late September 2016, which however, as outlined, did not get approval from the Senate.

Another major effort to perpetuate his policy of engagement came in mid-October 2016 when Obama issued a Presidential Policy Directive (PPD) on "United States-Cuba Normalization" (PPD-43). This directive, which according to Obama represented "another major step forward in our efforts to normalize relations with Cuba" (White House, 2016f), took stock of the administration's efforts to normalize the relationship with Cuba. It went out of its way to explicate that this policy has been driven by U.S. security and economic interests. The directive outlined "six U.S. objectives for the medium-term U.S.–Cuba relationship." Those included the further deepening of government-to-government relations, people-to-people interactions, and economic exchanges as well as measures aimed at contributing to political and economic reform in Cuba and the latter's integration in regional and global contexts.

The directive ended with a host of provisions on how to pursue and implement the aforementioned policy goals, which included suggestions for more than a dozen departments and agencies, such as defense, homeland security, interior, commerce, agriculture, and transportation (White House, 2016g). Since the outlined objectives were "medium-term" while Obama's second, thus final, term was about to end in around two months, the directive can only be seen as an effort to make it harder (albeit by no means impossible) for his successor to roll back the détente policy toward Cuba or, as Obama put it, to "make our opening to Cuba irreversible" (White House, 2016f). In this sense, one commentator referred to "a sweeping directive that will last beyond his [Obama's] presidency" whose aim was "to cement his administration's historic opening with Cuba" and to "transform[] what has been a presidential priority into a set of official mandates that will shape United States policy toward Cuba for decades" (Hirschfeld Davis, 2016c; similarly LeoGrande, 2016a: 33).

Just a few days before leaving office, Obama announced a few final measures aimed at removing vestiges of past U.S. policy on Cuba, thereby keeping up momentum for normalizing relations with Cuba until the very end of his administration. Crucially, the "wet foot, dry foot" policy that had been in place for more than 20 years was terminated (White House, 2017a).[15] The policy, which had been introduced by the Clinton administration in 1995, held that Cubans who reached U.S. soil ("dry foot") could stay and eventually apply for permanent residency while those who were stopped on the water ("wet foot") were returned to Cuba or a third state. Ending this in Obama's words "carryover of a [sic!] old way of thinking"—in the form of the special treatment that Cuban migrants received compared to migrants from "any other part of the world" (Obama, 2017)—was aimed primarily at curbing the number of economic refugees from Cuba. Since this goal was shared by the U.S. and Cuban governments, commentators considered the decision, or concession, as the administration's "final effort to normalize" relations with Cuba (Hirschfeld Davis and Robles, 2017). The measure to curb immigration was similarly considered an astute measure to make it harder for Obama's successor Donald Trump, who was critical of immigration, to roll back Obama's engagement policy (*The Economist*, 2017).

The deepening of the normalization process in the wake for the Cuba policy détente announcement through the adoption of a succession of measures was clearly helped by continued public support for the rapprochement. For example, respectively 63 percent and 73 percent of Americans supported Obama's announcement of re-establishing full diplomatic relations with Cuba as two Pew polls conducted in mid-January

2015, thus less than a month after Obama's "Cuba policy détente" speech, and July 2015 showed (Pew Research Center, 2015; Smith, 2016). Also, according to Gallup polls, Americans started to view Cuba in a much more favorable light, with 48 percent having a mostly/very favorable view in early 2015 and 54 percent in early 2016, which represented an increase of 20 points compared to 2013 and of even 33 points compared to 2006 (Norman, 2016).

Overall, then, Obama continuously and persistently added and expanded measures. Following initial steps during his first term, the process of normalizing relations gained significant momentum during the second term, as highlighted by—albeit by no means limited to—the major "Cuban policy détente" announcement and, in its wake, several meetings with President Castro, the reopening of embassies, the issuing of a Presidential Policy Directive (PPD-43), and the termination of the "wet foot, dry foot" policy. The empirical record therefore supports the expectation gleaned from Obama's personality trait scores that he did employ the tool of, thus engage in the scaling up of advocacy efforts in his attempt to introduce and implement a fundamental redirection in U.S. foreign policy toward Cuba.

Transforming institutions

Finally, Obama's trait scores suggested that he would try to transform institutions in his efforts to implement foreign policy change. This policy entrepreneurial instrument assumes that a leader is intimately familiar with the institutional environment within which he or she operates. In addition, and more demandingly, it suggests that a leader tries to adjust or adapt, thus ultimately manipulating said environment in his or her favor, thereby increasing the likelihood of the aspired foreign policy to come to fruition. This can be accomplished, for example, by increasing the representation of one's supporters in key decision-making institutions or by bypassing established channels of action if the leader perceives them as unconducive for the promotion of policy change. A leader could even try to fundamentally reform the institutional landscape altogether in his or her effort to usher in far-reaching policy changes, for example, by redefining the distribution of powers between his or her office and other institutions through constitutional changes. The empirical record suggests that while Obama did indeed try to alter the institutional environment within which he was operating—particularly with respect to Congress—he largely failed to accomplish this goal.

Obviously, Obama was patently aware of the institutional environment within which he was operating. Most tellingly, given a mostly recalcitrant Congress where no majority could be organized for his policy détente toward Cuba, Obama did—and in fact had no chance other than to—use his executive authority to advance unilaterally any changes in U.S.–Cuba policy. Above all, Congressional support would have been required to remove the most visible roadblock to normalization in the form of the embargo. As Obama stated: "With respect to Congress? We cannot unilaterally bring down the embargo" (Obama, 2014b).

Yet such Congressional action was not forthcoming. Relatedly, the president was barely in a position to increase the representation of supporters for his policy in Congress other than, say, by campaigning for them during House or Senate elections (for which, of course, Obama had to take into account numerous other policy areas as well). A fundamental general transformation of decision-making authority, thus the distribution of power, between the presidency and Congress based on constitutional reform was even more politically unfeasible.

This essentially confined Obama to modifying the effects of the embargo using his presidential authority and administrative actions on the one hand—of which he made ample use as outlined—and to calling on Congress to reconsider its position on the embargo on the other.[16] In terms of the latter, the following examples show that Obama repeatedly made recourse to such calls. For example, in his landmark "Cuba policy détente" announcement of December 2014, he invited Congress to have an "honest and serious debate about lifting the embargo" (Obama, 2014a). In the 2015 State of the Union address Obama similarly suggested that "Congress should begin work of ending the embargo" (White House, 2015a). Obama's later requests were even more explicit. For example, in his final State of the Union Address from January 2016 he declared:

> Fifty years of isolating Cuba had failed to promote democracy, and set us back in Latin America. That's why we restored diplomatic relations, opened the door to travel and commerce, positioned ourselves to improve the lives of the Cuban people. So if you want to consolidate our leadership and credibility in the hemisphere, recognize that the Cold War is over—lift the embargo. (White House, 2016a)

As a final example, Obama urged Congress to lift the embargo during his state visit to Cuba in March 2016: "And I will keep saying it every chance I get—one of the best ways to help the Cuban people succeed and improve their lives would be for the U.S. Congress to lift the embargo once and for all" (Obama, 2016c; also Obama, 2016e).

Obama also used international venues such as the United Nations General Assembly (UNGA) to put pressure on Congress to lift the embargo. In his 2015 speech before the UNGA Obama stated with respect to the rollout of his proposed policy changes that "As these contacts yield progress, I'm confident that our Congress will inevitably lift an embargo that should not be in place anymore" (White House, 2015d). Even more symbolically, the following year the United States abstained on a UNGA resolution that condemned the U.S. embargo against Cuba—rather than voting against such a resolution as the country had done the previous 25 years. The resolution was passed by a vote of 191 to zero with two abstentions, by the United States and Israel respectively. Commentators called this move, whose obvious main addressee was the U.S. Congress, "another important signal by the Obama administration of its intention to fully repair relations with Cuba, including an end to the embargo" (Sengupta and Gladstone, 2016).

Initially, Obama was hopeful that such calls coupled with his unilateral executive decisions might eventually move Congress in the (from his perspective) right direction. For example, a few days after his policy détente announcement, he stated:

> And what I do think is going to happen, though, is there's going to be a process where Congress digests it [Obama's policy détente announcement]. There are bipartisan supporters of our new approach, there are bipartisan detractors of this new approach. People will see how the actions we take unfold. And I think there's going to be a healthy debate inside of Congress. And I will certainly weigh in. (Obama, 2014b)

Closer to the end of his second term, during his state visit to Cuba, the president reiterated his hopes in Congressional action, albeit more cautiously. Importantly, he coupled his call with the acknowledgment that by then he had essentially exhausted his executive authority to ease the effects of the embargo so that any additional breakthrough had to come from Congress:

> But I'll be honest with you that the list of things that we can do administratively is growing shorter, and the bulk of changes that have to be made with respect to the embargo are now going to rely on Congress making changes. I've been very clear about the interests in getting that done before I leave. Frankly, Congress is not as productive as I would like during a Presidential election year. But the fact that we have such a large congressional delegation

with Democrats and Republicans with us is an indication that there is growing interest inside of Congress for lifting the embargo. (Obama, 2016d)

Ultimately, though, the president's hopes did not materialize. There was no majority in Congress to terminate the embargo, which accordingly remained in place.

While the question of lifting the embargo clearly was the most prominent issue where the president and Congress, or at least a majority therein, did not see eye to eye, it was by no means the only aspect of Obama's Cuba policy détente where disagreement existed. Indeed, as mentioned, already Obama's verbal pledges made during the 2008 presidential campaign to redirect U.S.–Cuba policy had been highly contentious. Thus, implementing such a policy after assuming the presidency had "the potential to become a political problem" (Shear, 2013) for Obama. Indeed, multiple elements of Obama's normalization policy did receive harsh criticism, as the following examples illustrate. Importantly, pushback against reform not only came from the Republican side but also from leading Democrats.

The fact that Obama lived up to his campaign promise of meeting up with the Cuban leadership presented an obvious hook for critique. This even included the brief handshake at the Mandela memorial service in late 2013. Republican Senator John McCain (R-AZ) not only saw no merit in this gesture by asking "What's the point?" He even likened it to the appeasement policy of the United Kingdom toward Adolf Hitler in the late 1930s by stating that British prime minister "Neville Chamberlain shook hands with Hitler" (AFP, 2013b). In a similar vein, the Cuban-born Republican Congress Women Ileana Ros-Lehtinen (R-FL) opined that "[S]ometimes a handshake is just a handshake, but when the leader of the free world shakes the bloody hand of a ruthless dictator like Raúl Castro, it becomes a propaganda coup for the tyrant" (AFP, 2013b).

Since already Obama's unintended encounter with Castro, which lasted just a few seconds, was met with such strong assessments, it came as little surprise that critics of Obama lambasted him for his pre-planned "actual" meetings as well. This was particularly true for Obama's state visit to Cuba in 2016. Indeed, critics already jumped on the very announcement of said visit. For example, Cuban-American Senator Robert Menendez (D-NJ) opined that "Despite the lack of reciprocity from a despotic and reinvigorated Castro regime, our president is rewarding this oppressive regime with a visit" (Hirschfeld Davis, 2016a). Cuban-American Senator Marco Rubio (R-FL) similarly chided Obama for his intention to travel to Cuba given the, from his viewpoint, at best limited reforms that the Cuban regime had undertaken so far in the course of the engagement policy: "Having an American president go to Cuba simply for the sake of going there, without the United States getting anything in return, is both counterproductive and damaging to our national security interests" (Hirschfeld Davis, 2016a). Critique continued during Obama's visit. For example, Cuban-American Senator Ted Cruz (R-TX), who ran for the 2016 Republican presidential nomination, argued that the president "has chosen to legitimize the corrupt and oppressive Castro regime with his presence on the island," adding that "sycophancy is having the effect is always does: It is telling our enemies that they can behave with impunity" (Cruz, 2016).

However, it was not only his personal meetings with Castro that his critics held against Obama. In addition, they reprimanded the president for numerous policy decisions as well. For example, in the run-up to the 2012 presidential elections, the eventual Republican nominee Mitt Romney chided Obama for handing out "gifts" to the Cuban leadership by removing restrictions on travel and money transfers (AP, 2012a) as well as for engaging in a "policy of appeasement" toward Cuba more broadly which "reward[ed] more despotism" (AP, 2012d). In a similar vein, Rubio derided Obama's approach to Cuba as outlined in the "Cuba policy détente" announcement as helping to perpetuate the survival of the Castro regime in Cuba rather than contributing to its ousting:

> This entire policy shift announced today is based on an illusion, on a lie, the lie and the illusion that more commerce and access to money and goods will translate to political freedom for the Cuban people ... All this is going to do is give the Castro regime, which controls every aspect of Cuban life, the opportunity to manipulate these changes to perpetuate itself in power. (Baker, 2014)

Menendez, who at that point chaired the Senate's Foreign Relations Committee, similarly placed little hope in Obama's approach to changing the situation in Cuba: "It is a fallacy that Cuba will reform just because the American president believes that if he extends his hand in peace, that the Castro brothers suddenly will unclench their fists" (Baker, 2014).

When the Obama administration eased restrictions on travel, monetary transactions, and commerce, Rubio challenged those measures not only on substantive grounds but called into question their legal foundation in the first place: "Not only do those measures harm the cause of a free Cuba, they also raise serious questions about the legality of the Obama administration's regulations" (Hirschfeld Davis, 2015b). Later, when seeking the Republican presidential nomination for 2016, Rubio referred to Obama's decision to formally re-establish diplomatic relations with Cuba as "a Faustian bargain that is contrary to our national values and also to our strategic interests" that only benefits "the ruling oligarchs" in Cuba instead of ordinary Cubans (Rubio, 2015). Consequently, Rubio was just as skeptical with respect to Obama's subsequent nomination of a U.S. ambassador to Cuba: "[R]ewarding the Castro government with a U.S. ambassador is another last-ditch legacy project for the president that needs to be stopped" (Hirschfeld Davis, 2016b)—and that in fact was stopped in Congress (see earlier). In turn, Menendez saw no merit in Obama's effort to remove Cuba from the state sponsors of terrorism list, suggesting that the administration's recommendation to that end "would represent another significant misstep in a misguided policy" (Hirschfeld Davis, 2015a). He similarly dismissed in harsh words Obama's last-minute decision to end the "wet foot, dry foot" policy which curtailed opportunities for Cubans to enter and permanently stay in the United States:

> Today's announcement will only serve to tighten the noose the Castro regime continues to have around the neck of its own people … The Obama administration seeks to pursue engagement with the Castro regime at the cost of ignoring the present state of torture and oppression, and its systematic curtailment of freedom. (Hirschfeld Davis and Robles, 2017)

The preceding illustrations show that Obama faced continued bipartisan pushback against a range of elements of his normalization policy with Cuba. In this sense, LeoGrande and Kornbluh (2014: 398) suggest that also during Obama's second term members of the Senate like Rubio and Menendez "were still determined to fight a legislative guerilla war against the president's Cuba policy by holding up nominations and threatening to filibuster must-pass legislation in order to block any new initiative." However, contrary to lifting the embargo and the appointment of an ambassador to Cuba for which Congressional approval was required, Obama was able to implement many other elements of his normalization policy toward Cuba by using his executive authority. So even without being able to transform the institutional environment within which he was operating, Obama did manage to implement significant policy changes.

Overall, then, Obama continuously tried to transform the institutional environment in which he was operating. He placed particular emphasis on winning over Congress for his policy of rapprochement toward Cuba. In the end, however, the president's efforts were in vain. He could not convince a sufficient number of members of Congress to follow his course, especially with regard to lifting the embargo. In turn, other, more coercive measures were simply not at his disposal, which left the institutional environment in terms of executive-legislative interactions in an unfavorable state from Obama's point of view. The only, albeit expected, exception in terms of actually (and from his view positively) shaping the institutional environment in support of his policy came in the form of Obama surrounding himself in his cabinet with advocates of his new approach (see the discussion on "bureaucratic pressure" in Chapter Four of this volume).

Conclusion

This chapter applied the leader-centered theory of foreign policy change to the case of U.S.–Cuba policy under the Obama administration. The discussions first showed that this case qualifies as an episode of major foreign policy change in that the Obama administration did usher in a fundamental redirection in U.S. foreign policy toward Cuba that came in the form "of a complex fabric" (LeoGrande, 2016b) of multiple decisions and actions covering a variety of issue areas. The ensuing changes far exceeded merely "incremental changes" that White (2015: 117) thought likely to occur given an uncooperative Congress. Indeed, changes came in both rhetoric ("words") and action ("deeds") and covered a range of substantive issue areas, as Hermann's definition of major foreign policy change expects.

In addition, the discussions also lend support to the theoretical expectations introduced in Chapter Two of this volume for each of the three stages of policy change. In terms of the initiation ("triggering change") of policy change, the preceding paragraphs have shown that Obama perceived

U.S.–Cuba policy as a major failure. This was particularly the case in terms of the programmatic dimension ("programmatic failure"). Indeed, he expressly and repeatedly highlighted shortcomings in American policy, which in his view were grounded in the use of inappropriate tools and strategies and thus all but inevitably produced low-quality policy outcomes. The latter concerned not only a failure in realizing American strategic interests toward Cuba and the region more broadly but also in improving the situation of ordinary Cubans. The discussion also showed that Obama was by no means alone in his diagnosis, which might have reinforced his views. Having said that, there was also considerable pushback against reversing course in U.S.–Cuba policy from both major parties. Still, for Obama his diagnosis of major policy failure pointed to the obvious need to fundamentally reorient U.S. policy. In so doing, the discussion lends support for expectation 1 which suggested that leaders who act as change agents publicly voice strong negative assessments of a current policy and call for fundamental revisions of that policy.

Concerning the substantive direction ("guiding change") of policy change, the expectations inferred from Obama's operational code (that is, political beliefs) about Cuba, and differences therein to the one of his predecessor George W. Bush, were indeed mirrored in the actual steps that he undertook to reorient U.S.–Cuba policy toward the island. Moving away from the conflictive policies undertaken by his predecessor, Obama took on a decidedly more cooperative stance toward Cuba as suggested by his operational code profile. The discussion thus lends support for expectations 2a and 2b. Those suggested that the political beliefs of leaders acting as change agents differ from the political beliefs of their predecessor and that the substantive direction in which leaders acting as change agents reorient their countries' foreign policy can be inferred from the differences between their political beliefs and the beliefs of their predecessor. True, political considerations cannot be dismissed as also being a factor. Still, the tenacity with which Obama pursued the rapprochement with Cuba over many years in combination with the timing of most of the key decision and actions in this regard suggest a predominant role of political beliefs in the president's efforts to usher in sweeping changes in U.S.–Cuba policy.

Finally, regarding the practical rollout ("implementing change") of policy change, Obama did make use of several policy entrepreneurial instruments in accordance with expectation 3a. What is more, the preceding discussion also suggests that the selection of entrepreneurial instruments can be tied to, thus seen as a function of, Obama's leadership traits as suggested by expectation 3b. High manifestations in the traits of, respectively, belief in the ability to control events, self-confidence, conceptual complexity, and need for power rendered the use of the policy entrepreneurial instruments of leading by example, scaling up advocacy efforts, and transforming institutions highly likely. The empirical record shows that Obama did indeed make consistent and extensive use of those instruments. While he ultimately failed to usher in a fundamental transformation of institutions, which meant above all that Congress did not heed his calls to end the embargo, Obama was nonetheless highly successful in ushering in the most far-reaching changes in U.S.–Cuba policy since the early 1960s by drawing on his executive authority. As Deputy National Security Advisor Rhodes put it: "We'd announced the farthest-reaching changes in U.S. policy *that the law would allow*" (Rhodes, 2019: 352; emphasis added). Overall, then, the discussion suggests that Obama did indeed have an independent, systematic, and predictable effect on fundamentally redirecting U.S. policy toward Cuba, where he ushered in a process of normalization in the bilateral relationship after decades of conflict.

FOUR

Alternative Explanations

The previous chapter showed that President Obama played a key role for bringing about fundamental changes in U.S.–Cuba policy. By extension, it suggested that said change was the result of individual agency and leadership. However, as the literature review in Chapter One of this volume has highlighted, the Foreign Policy Analysis (FPA) scholarship on foreign policy change generally places a premium on structural factors as representing the main drivers or causes of change. In a similar vein, in his specific discussion of U.S.–Cuba policy under Obama, LeoGrande (2015b: 488) refers to a set of structural factors, and changes therein, that opened up a policy window for far-reaching changes in U.S. policy. From those vantage points, Obama was not the driver of change but was rather being driven by structural factors to usher in policy change. In the final analysis, a structural perspective would suggest that any person who held the presidency from 2009 onward would have introduced far-reaching changes since it was not agent-related but structural factors that underpinned the process of change.

Against this background, the following discussion zooms in on three structural factors located on different levels of analysis that are frequently emphasized in the FPA literature as important for bringing about policy change. Those are:

- international pressure;
- bureaucratic pressure; and
- societal pressure.

The discussion explores the extent to which those factors offer similar or even better explanations of the fundamental changes in U.S.–Cuba policy during the Obama administration than the one based on the leader-centered theory of foreign policy change presented in the previous chapter.

International pressure

One explanatory factor for foreign policy change frequently mentioned in the literature concerns external pressure on a country to change course (for example, Gustavsson, 1999). More often than not, external pressure is exerted by more powerful states against less powerful ones. In such hierarchical contexts, the powerful states demand that the less powerful states redirect their policies in order to align them with their own goals and interests. Another source for changing course could be external shocks. Yet there is little evidence that U.S.–Cuba policy under Obama changed for any of those reasons.

To be clear, this is not to say that U.S.–Cuba policy received widespread support or followership. Indeed, the literature shows an ebb and flow of support for U.S. sanctions policy against Cuba. This included the country's European allies who, for example, "grudgingly cooperated" with the Americans in the 1960s but were quite critical of the tightening of the sanctions regime in the 1990s (LeoGrande, 2015a: 948, 946). As a result, U.S. leadership in sanctioning Cuba generated only limited followership. What is more, it was often met by critique, not least from countries from the Global South where many states "empathized" with Cuba (Guiliano, 1998: 183).

However, a lack of sustained support for or outright critique of U.S. sanctions policy against Cuba is by no means synonymous with the existence of any meaningful and consequential international pressure on the United States that would have caused the country to change course. As stated before, for external pressure to lead to policy changes, this typically requires hierarchical power relations between actors, with the stronger imposing its views on the weaker. Yet U.S. power after the end of the Cold War and the ensuing "unipolar moment" (Krauthammer, 1990/1991) was second to none. As result, there simply was no other actor or group of actors that could have pressured the United States into reversing its policy. This was also true for the final years of the George W. Bush administration when Obama started to voice his goal of normalizing relations with Cuba during the 2008 presidential campaign and the first years of the Obama administration in the run-up to the 2014 "Cuba policy détente" declaration.

In short, sustained external critique from other states or international organizations on U.S.–Cuba policy had not triggered any meaningful adaptation, let alone a reversal in said policy before Obama assumed the presidency. There is similarly no indication that Obama's decision to change course was driven or caused by external pressure. While the president was also confronted with external critique personally, for example, during the Summit of the Americas in 2009 and 2012 respectively, it seems far-fetched to assume that he budged to this critique and therefore decided to change course. Rather, much more narrowly, Obama was cognizant of the lack of external support for U.S.–Cuba policy and included this fact in his diagnosis of the situation, which was not satisfactory also for several other reasons (see the discussion on "triggering change"). So rather than being pressured into action by external critique, he incorporated it into his considerations and also used it as justification for his envisaged policy reversal.

Similarly, there is little support that the change in policy was caused by external shocks. After all, change did not occur after the seismic shift in international politics that the collapse of the Soviet Union represented. Rather, it came more than 20 years later, following a somewhat thawing in U.S. policy toward Cuba during the Clinton administration and a re-hardening during the George W. Bush administration. Last, the intra-family transition in the Cuban leadership from Fidel

Castro to his brother Raúl hardly qualifies as an external shock in the first place.

Bureaucratic pressure

Another often-mentioned driver of foreign policy change is bureaucratic pressure (for example, Hermann, 1990). The underlying idea is that certain ministries or other types of bureaucratic entities (agencies, and so on) are dissatisfied and therefore call for a reorientation of policy. As per the "bureaucratic politics model," such demands are rooted in the organizational interests of the respective ministries who vie for competencies and resources with other ministries. The representatives of the ministries, whose policy preferences are held to be determined by their bureaucratic position as per the adage "Where you stand depends on where you sit," engage in inter-ministerial bargaining or the "pulling and hauling that is politics" (Allison and Zelikow, 1999: 307, 255). If the advocates of change prevail, adjustments of policy follow.

Yet there is little indication that bureaucratic politics drove the Obama administration's reversal of the Cuba policy. For starters, Obama had already voiced his ideas of "normalizing" relations with Cuba during the campaign trail (see Chapter Three of this volume), thus before becoming formally involved in inter-ministerial bargaining processes. Later, after assuming the presidency, Obama lived up to his campaign promises by implementing a fundamental change in U.S.–Cuba policy. Thus, there is no indication, and in fact also no need, that bureaucratic pressure would have caused Obama to engage in a fundamental overhaul of U.S. policy toward Cuba, since this is something that he already had in mind anyway.

If anything, bureaucratic politics could have become meaningful in the opposite direction, in the sense of representing obstacles for Obama in his endeavor to redirect U.S. policy toward Cuba. Yet there is also little empirical evidence for this. On the contrary, key members of the administration supported

Obama's redirection (Kornbluh and LeoGrande, 2019: 19–22). This also included Obama's first secretary of state, Hillary Rodham Clinton, who, while being critical of Obama's plans during the presidential campaign, supported this policy after assuming office (for example, AFP, 2009).

The same can be said for Clinton's successor as secretary of state, John Kerry, during whose tenure the far-reaching changes occurred. Kerry had already been "an outspoken critic of Washington's policy on Cuba while in the Senate" (AP, 2013). Accordingly, after taking over the post of secretary of state in the second Obama administration, Kerry's buy-in into Obama's goal of changing course came as little surprise (see also Kerry, 2018: 424–9). For example, during the flag raising ceremony at the U.S. embassy in Havana in August 2015 Kerry stated: "[W]e are gathered here today because our leaders—President Obama and President Castro—made a courageous decision to stop being the prisoners of history and to focus on the opportunities of today and tomorrow" (U.S. Department of State, 2015).

Similar statements of support for a policy reversal and specific measures required to put this reversal into practice came from other members of the administration as well. For example, U.S. Secretary of the Treasury Jacob Lew emphasized in September 2015 with respect to recently introduced measures by his department and the Commerce Department in terms of travel, remittances, and commerce that "By further easing these sanctions, the United States is helping to support the Cuban people in their effort to achieve the political and economic freedom necessary to build a democratic, prosperous, and stable Cuba" (Hirschfeld Davis, 2015b). Support also extended to the advisory staff where, for example, Deputy National Security Advisor for Strategic Communications Ben Rhodes played a pivotal role in the back-channel process that was set up in mid-2013 and that paved the way for the Cuba policy détente announcement the following year (for example, DeYoung, 2016).[1]

Overall, there is no indication that bureaucratic pressure was the key driver for the fundamental changes in U.S.–Cuba policy during the Obama administration. There simply was no need to convince Obama to engage in such change since he himself had already proposed it before assuming the presidency. There is similarly no indication that the reverse effect of bureaucratic pressure, in the form of stalling change, played a role since there seemed to have been wide support within the administration for the normalization process.

Societal pressure

A third possible source for foreign policy change can emerge from society (for example, Hermann, 1990). If societal groups are dissatisfied with certain policies, they can try to exert pressure on a leader to alter course. Such pressure is particularly likely to succeed if the leader needs the societal group in order to survive in office.

Indeed, Americans showed an openness toward redirecting U.S. foreign policy toward Cuba in more cooperative directions (see Chapter Three of this volume). For example, repeated Gallup polls starting in the late 1990s showed that a majority supported the reopening of diplomatic relations with Cuba, reaching 67 percent in 2006. A majority of Americans also favored ending the trade embargo (Gallup, n.d.). Similarly, in nationwide polls conducted in 2009, 71 percent of Americans were supportive of re-establishing full diplomatic relations, and 64 percent wanted to see an easing of travel restrictions (CNN, 2009).

Maybe more surprisingly still, the sizable Cuban community in Florida, which tended to be conservative and anti-Castro—LeoGrande (2015: 959) refers to this group as "the traditional stronghold of conservative rejectionists"—showed signs of support for adjusting U.S.–Cuba policy. For example, in a 2008 poll among that group that was conducted after the presidential elections, two-thirds of the respondents favored lowering restrictions on sending money to Cuba, thus turning back changes ushered in by the Bush administration in 2003. The same number supported a return to the less stringent pre-2003 travel policy. The poll further showed majorities in favor of ending the embargo and for re-establishing diplomatic relations between the two countries. Also, 80 percent of the respondents favored direct talks between the two governments (all data from FIU, 2008).

Follow-up polls among Cuban Americans living in Florida that were conducted before Obama made the landmark "Cuba policy détente" announcement in 2011 and 2014 respectively[2] showed similar levels of support. For example, there continued to be majorities for establishing diplomatic relations, unrestricted travel to Cuba for all Americans, and the expansion of economic ties. The picture became less clear-cut regarding the continuation of the embargo, though, which was favored by 56 percent of the respondents in 2011 but only 48 percent in 2014 (FIU, 2011, 2014). Importantly, more than 50 percent of the respondents in those polls were registered as Republican voters, which suggests that among the Cuban community in Florida changing course in U.S.–Cuba policy was by no means confined to supporters of the Democrats (FIU, 2008, 2011, 2014).

Overall, then, there clearly was societal pressure, or at least demand, to redirect U.S.–Cuba policy. However, societal pressure alone cannot explain the fundamental redirection as ushered in by the Obama administration for several reasons. For starters, a key actor in this context, in form of Cuban Americans, offered no clear guidance in this regard. This group traditionally tended to advocate isolating, coercing, and eventually toppling the Castro regime (for example, Pérez, 2014: 132, 140–1), which obviously would not have favored the kind of policy change that Obama eventually pursued. Having said that, younger Cuban Americans were considerably less hostile and thus more open to a change in U.S. policy to more cooperative directions, as indicated by numerous opinion polls at the time (for example, FIU, 2008, 2014). Overall, then, the Cuban-American community did not offer a clear impetus for policy adjustments. On the contrary, the divergence in strategic objectives within the Cuban-American community as well as between the older, conservative part of said community and the Obama administration contributed to the group's "receding ... political clout" (Haney, 2018: 167) more generally. In this sense, LeoGrande (2020: 449) calls Obama's 2014 policy détente announcement "a profound defeat for the [conservative] Cuba lobby"—which is a far cry away from assuming that said lobby drove the policy change as introduced by the Obama administration.

In terms of U.S. society more broadly, these numbers show that Americans in general were open to seeing U.S. policy change already throughout the 2000s. Yet neither this general trend nor the more specific fact that supporters of the Republicans (including Cuban Americans) were open to changes as well, made President George W. Bush redirect U.S.–Cuba policy during his tenure. If anything, the opposite happened, as exemplified by the tightening of travel restrictions and remittance flows in 2003.

Further, as shown in Chapter Three of this volume, during the 2008 presidential campaign Obama stood essentially alone among the main contenders from both major parties with his call for a fundamental redirection of U.S. foreign policy toward Cuba. In other words, similar to sitting President Bush, neither Republican John McCain nor Democrat Hillary Rodham Clinton picked up in any meaningful way societal demands for fundamentally altering American policy in more cooperative directions. Thus counterfactually, had either of them won the presidency, policy adjustments, particularly to the extent to which Obama first advocated and later implemented them, would have been very unlikely to happen.[3]

Last, the policy of Obama's immediate successor Donald Trump similarly shows that, independent from societal views, a more cooperative posture toward Cuba has by no means become a bipartisan consensus in Washington. Indeed, Trump reversed many of the changes initiated by the Obama administration (see Chapter Five of this volume) *despite* continued support for a host of measures initiated by his predecessor. The latter included Cuban Americans in Florida who, according to polls taken in 2016 and 2018 respectively, supported Obama's decisions, for example, with respect to re-establishing full diplomatic relations, deepening economic ties, and lifting travel restrictions (FIU, 2016, 2018).

In short, then, societal demands did indeed favor a reorientation of U.S.–Cuba policy in more cooperative directions, as was eventually introduced by the Obama administration. At the same time, they alone cannot explain the timing of when said change happened (under Obama rather than, say, Bush), nor for that matter the reversal of some of the changes ushered in by the Obama administration under his successor Donald Trump. In other words, societal pressures seem to have served neither as a necessary nor sufficient condition for policy change but rather, more narrowly, as an incentive that leaders may, or may not, act upon.

Conclusion

The preceding discussion offers very little empirical support for any of the three structural factors that are frequently cited in the FPA literature on foreign policy change to have played a role in bringing about fundamental changes in U.S.–Cuba policy during the Obama administration. In terms of external pressure, there simply was no sufficiently powerful state or international organization that could have made the United States change course. Regarding bureaucratic pressure, there was no need to convince Obama to change course since this had already been his goal upon assuming the presidency. And while there was indeed societal pressure to or at least societal interest in altering U.S.–Cuba policy, this factor alone falls short of accounting for the timing, scope, and also lack of durability of the changes introduced by Obama. Together, this lack of empirical support for the three alternative structural explanations provides further backing for the plausibility of the leader-centered explanation presented in Chapter Three of this volume.

FIVE

Conclusion and Outlook

This book introduced a leader-centered theory of foreign policy change and applied said theory to examine changes in U.S.–Cuba policy during the Obama administration. This concluding section proceeds in three steps. It first summarizes the argument of the book. It then briefly explores the extent to which the proposed theory can account for additional changes, in the form of reversals of Obama's policy changes, that were introduced by his successor Donald Trump. The discussion concludes with avenues for future research.

Summary of the argument

Leaders are commonly associated with and held responsible for fundamental changes in the foreign policy of their countries. In this sense, George W. Bush started the war in Iraq, Chinese foreign policy became much more coercive under Xi Jinping, and Vladimir Putin decided to invade Ukraine. However, and somewhat surprisingly, the academic literature on foreign policy change has so far placed limited emphasis on the role of leaders as key agents of policy change. This is not to say that leaders have been ignored altogether. However, as outlined in Chapter One of this volume, analytical frameworks typically combine a host of both structural and actor-oriented factors in their explanations of episodes of major foreign policy change. What is largely missing are frameworks that would allow to discern any independent, systematic, and predictable effect of individual leaders on such processes.

A LEADER-CENTERED THEORY OF FOREIGN POLICY CHANGE

To that end, this volume has introduced a "leader-centered theory of foreign policy change" in Chapter Two which seeks to account for major changes in a country's foreign policy. Following the definition of Charles Hermann (1990), such kinds of changes do not come in one-off decisions nor are they confined to a specific issue area but rather comprise substantial changes in both rhetoric and actions, include a succession of decisions, and span multiple issue areas. The theory suggests that leaders have a systematic, independent, and predictable effect on the substance and the direction of such processes. Those effects concern the "why," "what," and "how" of foreign policy change.

The "why" relates to the reasons why leaders seek to fundamentally reorient their countries' foreign policy ("triggering change"), which the theory connects to leaders' diagnosis of failure of existing policies. The "what" concerns the substantive direction in which leaders seek to reorient policy ("guiding change"), which the theory conceives as a function of the political beliefs that leaders have with respect to the policy in question. Finally, the "how" refers to the actions that leaders undertake to put into practice the aspired policy change ("implementing change"), where the theory ties the use of policy entrepreneurial instruments by leaders to their leadership traits. While those three dimensions or stages are interrelated in practice, they can be kept separate for analytical purposes. To operationalize the effect of leaders along those three dimensions, the theory incorporates insights from the fields of Foreign Policy Analysis (FPA), in the form of Operational Code Analysis and Leadership Trait Analysis, and public policy, in the form of the literatures on policy failures and policy entrepreneurship.

The book uses the leader-centered theory of foreign policy change to explain changes in U.S. foreign policy toward Cuba under the Obama administration in Chapter Three. While this episode is widely perceived as representing a fundamental shift in U.S. policy, it has so far received scant attention in theory-driven foreign policy scholarship. Moreover, there is no clear position in the literature in terms of Obama's specific role in this context. The analysis of the case through the lens of the leader-centered theory suggests that President Obama did indeed play a major role in "replac[ing] a Cold War framework of animosity with a twenty-first-century policy of engagement and cooperation" (LeoGrande, 2015b: 486).

Specifically, Obama deemed American policy toward Cuba a blatant failure, which he sought to rectify by pursuing a policy of rapprochement, or normalization, toward Cuba in accordance with his political beliefs. To that end, he engaged in a variety of policy entrepreneurial actions, such as leading by example or scaling up advocacy efforts, the use of which was indicated by his leadership traits. As result, U.S. foreign policy toward Cuba underwent the most fundamental changes since the early 1960s. This is not to deny that the rollout of Obama's policy of normalization encountered a host of practical challenges, not only on the Cuban side but also domestically in the United States, for example, in the form of a recalcitrant Congress.[1] However, rather than calling into question the fundamental nature of policy change or the president's role therein, those challenges arose only because of the major redirection that Obama was able to usher in as highlighted by the leader-centered theory.

Still, given the common emphasis in the literature on foreign policy change on structural factors, this volume has explored alternative explanations for the case under examination in Chapter Four. The alternatives referred to international pressure, bureaucratic pressure, and societal pressure as possible drivers of major changes in U.S.–Cuba policy. However, the discussions found little empirical support for any of those factors. No other actor pressured the United States to alter course. Also, key bureaucratic actors supported Obama's policy of normalization, as did larger parts of American society including an increasing number of Cuban Americans. Those by and large non-findings lend further support for the plausibility of leader-centered explanation.

U.S.–Cuba policy under Trump

U.S.–Cuba policy also lends itself to an initial stab at probing the external validity of the leader-centered theory, in terms of its explanatory power for additional cases in form of the Cuba policy of Donald Trump. As fundamental as the changes introduced by him were, Obama was patently aware that there was no guarantee that his successor would continue his policy of engagement with Cuba. Therefore, Obama's goal was to advance the process of normalization as far as possible during his period in office, thereby making policy change "irreversible" (White House, 2016f). Close to the end of his term, Obama was hopeful that this would actually be the case, stating that "I don't anticipate major changes in policy from the new [Trump] administration" (Obama, 2016h). Yet the actions of the Trump administration showed that Obama's domestic political goal, or hope, was not to materialize.[2]

Just like Obama had done before him, Trump used his executive authority to remove or undo many of the changes that his predecessor had introduced (for details, see White House, 2019; Laguardia Martinez et al, 2020: 98–104; Sullivan, 2022: 10–13), thereby seeking to "cancel[] the last administration's completely one-sided deal with Cuba" (Trump, 2017). Indeed, Trump wasted little time in bringing about change, with several decisions and actions connected to the "readjustment of the United States policy towards Cuba" (White House, 2017b) already coming less than six months into his presidency. Those initial decisions were outlined in National Security Presidential Memorandum NSPM–5 entitled "Strengthening the Policy of the United States toward Cuba." They aimed primarily at the reintroduction of stricter measures regarding travel, trade, and the flow of remittances to Cuba (White House, 2017c). Restrictions in those areas were tightened further in September 2020 in the run-up to the presidential election (Trump, 2020).

Further decisions to reverse course included a significant drawdown of personnel at the U.S. embassy in Cuba. While Trump had originally pledged to keep the U.S. embassy in Havana open during his major Cuba policy announcement of June 2017 (Trump, 2017), just a few months later all "nonessential staff" were removed in response to the "Havana syndrome."[3] The following year then saw the suspension of consular services at the embassy (Laguardia Martinez et al, 2020: 63). Also, rather than using the United Nations General Assembly (UNGA) to put pressure on Congress to lift the trade embargo as Obama had done, the Trump administration returned to voting in opposition to (rather than abstaining) an annual resolution against the embargo (Gladstone, 2017). In addition, Trump actively moved against the Castro regime by tightening sanctions against Venezuela (White House, 2019), whose president, Nicolás Maduro, he described as being "not a Venezuelan patriot; he is a Cuban puppet" (Trump, 2019). Last but not least, in mid-January 2021, hence just a few days before the Trump administration ended, Cuba was reinstated to the state sponsors of terrorism list (U.S. Embassy in Cuba, 2021).

While Trump did not completely erase or reverse all of the changes that Obama had ushered in, his decisions and actions unquestionably introduced yet another fundamental change in U.S.–Cuba policy, which amounted to "a deliberate attempt to dismantle Obama's legacy" (Anderson, 2017). Crucially for the argument of this book, the episode also highlights the key role that individual decision makers can have in redirecting foreign policy. As a result of Trump's "re-reversal" of Obama's policy reversal, U.S.–Cuba policy became much more confrontational again, just like it had been before Obama had taken over the presidency, thereby ushering in an "antagonistic freeze in the Cuba-U.S. relationship" (Laguardia Martinez et al, 2020: 101).

It is not possible to engage in a full-fledged empirical analysis of Trump's Cuba policy in this concluding chapter; however, the theoretical framework proposed in this volume would suggest that for such a redirection to occur, Trump should have considered Obama's policy of engagement a failure, with his political beliefs pointing to a more confrontational posture, and that he should have selected policy entrepreneurial instruments in accordance with his leadership traits to bring about such change. Overall, the following paragraphs point to initial empirical support for those expectations.

In terms of diagnosing failure, Trump was indeed critical of Obama's approach toward Cuba, and arguably increasingly so. At first, he suggested that the opening policy of Obama was "fine" but that "we should have made a stronger deal." Later in the presidential campaign, though, he changed his position, suggesting that the Obama administration made "concessions" that "the next president can reverse" (all quotes from Diamond, 2016). After assuming office, Trump was even more outspoken in his negative evaluation of Obama's Cuba policy. For example, in his major announcement concerning a reversal in policy toward Cuba in June 2017, he opined: "It's hard to think of a policy that makes less sense than the prior administration's terrible and misguided deal with the Castro regime" (Trump, 2017). Similarly, in his 2020 State of the Union Address, Trump lauded his administration for "revers[ing] the failing policies of the previous administration on Cuba" (White House, 2020). Later that year, in a speech that honored veterans of the Bay of Pigs invasion, Trump similarly stated that "The Obama-Biden administration made a weak, pathetic, one-sided deal with the Castro dictatorship that betrayed the Cuban people and enriched the communist regime" (Trump, 2020). In short, Trump was clearly critical of Obama's Cuba policy, which according to the leader-centered theory served as a trigger for reversing course.

In terms of guiding change, a decidedly tentative profile of the Cuba beliefs of Trump (see Appendix 1) and its comparison with the Cuba beliefs of Obama brings to the fore several differences. For example, Trump had a somewhat more conflictual perception of the political environment concerning Cuba, and he was more pessimistic in terms of realizing his goals, though both results were not statistically significant. However, the latter was the case with regard to the dimension of words/deeds, where Trump should have been considerably less flexible than Obama. He should have similarly placed much less emphasis on the utility of offering rewards. Finally, Cuba policy appeared more predictable for Trump than it had been for Obama, with an ensuing more limited role of chance. Jointly, those differences offer indications that Trump should have indeed opted for a more confrontational policy compared to his predecessor and, in doing so, "cancel[] the Obama-Biden sellout to the Castro regime" (Trump, 2020).

In terms of implementing change, Trump's LTA profile (see Table A.1 in the Appendix) suggests that he should have been particularly likely to engage in scaling up advocacy efforts. This expectation seems to be corroborated by the empirical evidence. Indeed, just like Obama had done, Trump also did not roll out his reversal of U.S.–Cuba policy in a one-off decision but rather set a first mark early in his tenure and subsequently added additional measures to further advance policy change. In addition, the profile provides somewhat ambiguous expectations in terms of team building. While a low task focus means that Trump should have been willing to include others in his policy making, the extremely high level of distrust suggests that any delegation should have been limited to a very small core group around him. Trump's close consultations, for example, with Senator Rubio or the fact that it was Vice President Mike Pence who represented the United States at the 8th Summit of the Americas in April 2018 in Lima, Peru, could be indications for this (White House, 2018).

Obviously the preceding paragraphs offer merely an initial sketch of what the application of the leader-centered theory of policy change to the case of U.S.–Cuba policy under Donald Trump—who "largely revers[ed] Barack Obama's opening to the island" (*The Economist*, 2021)—might entail. Also, alternative accounts suggest that other factors than political beliefs might have played an important role in Trump's policy reversal, ranging from his general transactional, business-oriented mindset (for example, LeoGrande, 2016b) to electoral concerns (for example, Haney, 2018: 176). Still, there seems to be sufficient initial support to warrant closer examination. This is also the bridge to the final section of this volume, which outlines avenues for future research.

Suggestions for future research

This book has provided initial support for the proposed leader-centered theory of foreign policy change, which offered a plausible account of the major redirection of U.S. policy toward Cuba under Barack Obama. The brief sketch outlined suggests that the theory might be similarly helpful in explaining the re-reversal of U.S.–Cuba policy under Trump. Having said that, the preceding discussions have also pointed to several avenues for extensions and refinements of the theoretical framework.

For starters, the proposed theory is not meant to be deterministic, in the sense that each instance in which a leader criticizes a certain policy will eventually lead to major foreign policy change. In other words, while the diagnosis of a badly failing or failed policy is necessary for major policy change to occur, the assumption is not that such diagnosis translates automatically into such an outcome. Future research should thus explore the conditions under which a diagnosis of policy failure may or may not lead to foreign policy change, which would also be a hook to bring back the work on foreign policy "stabilizers" (Goldmann, 1982). A lack of change may result, for example, from a leader's inability to come up with a viable policy alternative. Further, a leader might be predisposed (due to his or her set of traits) to employ policy entrepreneurial instruments that are inappropriate for putting into practice the aspired foreign policy change. More broadly, a leader might lack key attributes of policy entrepreneurs (for example, ambition, social acuity, sociability, and tenacity) (Mintrom, 2020: 8–10) to take on such a role in the first place. Last, critique could be voiced for purely instrumental reasons rather than grounded in conviction, and is therefore not followed up. An identical outcome would emerge if a leader decides that notwithstanding a policy's failure, the issue is not politically salient enough to invest political capital to bring about change.

Briefly returning to the case of U.S. policy toward Cuba, the Biden administration seems to be an example of a "non-case" (see, for example, LeoGrande, 2023). On the one hand, Biden, who was Vice President during the Obama administration and thus involved (albeit not prominently) in the normalization process during that period, left little doubt about his negative assessment of Trump's Cuba policy. For example, he suggested that the Trump "administration's approach is not working" (Glueck, 2020) and pledged to "reverse the failed Trump policies that inflicted harm on Cubans and their families" (Sesin, 2020). However, in this case a diagnosis of failure did not lead to yet another major reversal in U.S. policy. While Biden eased some of the measures introduced by Trump, for example, concerning travel and remittances and also re-staffed the U.S. embassy in Havana, he maintained several other policies of Trump, such as Cuba's designation as state sponsor of terrorism or the no-vote in the UNGA on the resolution to lift the embargo (for example, White House, 2021a; CRS, 2022). He even imposed additional sanctions against Cuba in response to a governmental crackdown against protestors in July 2021 (White House, 2021b). Overall, then, "Biden's policy was not substantially different than Trump's" (LeoGrande, 2023: 223), which is why commentators suggested that Biden followed "a Trump-lite approach with Cuba" (Barrett, 2023).

Returning to open conceptual questions, what if leaders, responding to a blatant policy failure, have to redirect a policy that was not introduced by one of their predecessors but by themselves? In such situations, the "choice dilemma" in terms of staying the course or changing policy (Hermann, 2012b: 3) should be even more pronounced since redirecting one's own policies would entail even greater political and arguably also psychological costs. Thus, in which ways do such contexts of responsibility and possibly also "culpability" (Croco, 2011) impede the diagnosis of failure on the part of leaders, which has been suggested as the key trigger for initiating processes of change?

Finally, it goes without saying that future applications of the leader-centered theory of foreign policy change must not be confined to one political system. Rather, studies should move beyond the presidential democracy of the United States, for example, by including cases of major foreign policy change from parliamentary democracies, where, for instance, coalition governance might add a further layer of complexity. In addition, cases from non-democratic systems should be examined through the lens of the theory. An obvious candidate would be to explore the role of Raúl Castro in pursuing normalization with the United States. Such a study would not only complement this book's discussion but would have the additional upside of providing a non-Western case to the study of foreign policy change.[4]

APPENDIX 1

Trump's Political Beliefs on Cuba

As a caveat: The following profile of Donald Trump rests on just two speeches. The simple reason for this is that those two speeches were the only ones that I could identify that President Trump gave during this tenure in office specifically on Cuba (Trump, 2017, 2020). Since political beliefs are held to be issue-specific, additional speeches in which Trump discussed, for

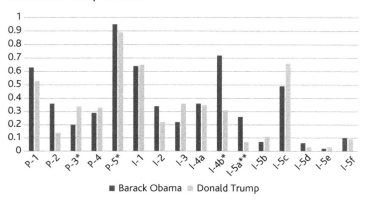

Figure A.1: Comparison of the political beliefs of U.S. presidents Obama and Trump on Cuba

Note: Two-tailed t-tests (* significant at .10; ** significant at .05)

example, Venezuela (at times with only occasional references to Cuba) or Latin America more generally were not included. The two speeches at hand comprise a total of some 5,400 words. As a result, the text source for the profile does not meet Operational Code Analysis convention, which must be taken into account in the interpretation of the results. See Chapter Three for details on Obama's profile.

APPENDIX 2

Expectations for Donald Trump as Policy Entrepreneur

As per Leadership Trait Analysis convention, the following profile of Donald Trump is based on 100 spontaneous statements comprising some 52,000 words. The statements were made in front of different audiences, cover different substantive areas, and come from different phases of his tenure in office.

Table A.1: Trump's leadership traits

Decision makers Trait	Trump	Anglo-American norming group (n=15)	Z scores	Trump *compared* to Anglo-American norming group	Expectation for policy entrepreneurial action
Belief in the ability to control events (BACE)	.39	.36 (.04)	0.75	Average	n/a
Self-confidence (SC)	.50	.45 (.08)	0.625	Average	n/a
Conceptual complexity (CC)	.65	.60 (.05)	**1.0**	**High**	**Engage in scaling up advocacy efforts**
Need for power (PWR)	.24	.24 (.04)	0	Average	n/a
Task focus (TASK)	.54	.62 (.06)	**-1.33**	**Low**	**Ambiguous re. team-building** (low TASK should render it more likely while extremely high DIS should render use of teams beyond core group highly unlikely)
Distrust of others (DIS)	.27	.12 (.03)	**5.0**	**Extremely high**	
In-group bias (IGB)	.15	.13 (.03)	.67	Average	n/a

Note: Z scores based on comparison of Trump's scores with Anglo-American norming group. Standard deviations in parenthesis

Source: Own compilation using data from Fouquet and Brummer (2023)

Notes

one Introduction

[1] Obama (2015c).
[2] Other factors listed are economic opportunities, security concerns, transcultural ties, as well as regional and global policy goals of the United States.
[3] While LeoGrande's article also briefly taps into a few works on policy change from both public policy (that is, Kingdon, 2011) and FPA (that is, Welch, 2005) that are also referenced in this volume, no individual theory is expressly driving the empirical analysis, nor are there efforts to combine different perspectives into a broader theoretical framework.
[4] Jürgen Haacke (2021) examines an episode of foreign policy change initiated by the Obama administration through the lens of policy entrepreneurship, the latter of which also plays a role in the leader-centered theory proposed in this book. However, his article focuses on U.S. policy toward Myanmar rather than Cuba, and it does not connect policy entrepreneurial actions to individual leaders' political beliefs or leadership traits.

two A Leader-Centered Theory of Foreign Policy Change

[1] Moving the discussion from the initiation of policy change to the likely success of such endeavors, Gustavsson (1999: 86) opines that the latter "will be enhanced if this can be tied to a crisis of some kind."
[2] James Walsh (2006) similarly establishes a connection between the existence of policy failure and policy change, which depends on the availability of viable policy alternatives. The proposed leader-centered theory suggests that such policy alternatives result from leaders' beliefs.
[3] For a different perspective that calls for a clear-cut separation between policy entrepreneurs(hip) and leaders(hip), see Capano and Galanti (2018).
[4] As outlined in greater detail in Chapter One, while also connecting LTA or rather the trait "conceptual complexity" to foreign policy change, Yang's article does not embed the argument in a broader conceptual framework (Yang, 2010).
[5] The "norming group" data is available from *Social Science Automation* (https://socialscience.net/).
[6] On "theory-testing case studies," see George and Bennett (2005: 75, 109), and on "no-variance designs" and case selection on the dependent

variable, see the work by Mahoney and colleagues who suggest that "case selection is a model-dependent issue; one must select cases that allow one to test the empirical implications of the hypothesis being tested" (Goertz and Mahoney, 2012: 181), which in turn could serve as a point of departure "for broader comparative studies and new hypotheses" (Collier and Mahoney, 1996: 74).

three U.S. Foreign Policy Change toward Cuba under Obama

[1] Obama (2014a).
[2] Cuba also released more than 50 political prisoners shortly after the announcements by the two presidents, as had been discussed during the secret back channel talks beforehand (Rhodes, 2019: 287).
[3] Like Obama did on multiple occasions, Castro emphasized in his statement both continued challenges (for example, "This in no way means that the heart of the matter has been resolved") and positive developments (for example, "[T]he progress made in our exchanges proves that it is possible to find solutions to many problems") (Baker 2014). Later, during a joint press conference between him and Obama in Panama City in March 2015, Castro similarly emphasized that both sides "have agreed to disagree" while also suggesting the possibility of "a friendship between our two peoples" (White House, 2015b).
[4] This is not to say that there was no political support at all for Obama's suggestion to redirect U.S. policy toward Cuba, which was supported, for example, by his future secretary of state, John Kerry, who, as Democratic nominee for the 2004 election, had already clashed with sitting President George W. Bush over Cuba policy (for example, AFP, 2004).
[5] The OCA coding scheme is available at profilerplus.org.
[6] The LTA coding scheme is available at profilerplus.org.
[7] The first Summit of the Americas was held in Miami, USA, in 1994.
[8] This was the first time that Raúl Castro addressed the UNGA. Like Obama did a few hours before him (White House, 2015d), Castro also called on the U.S. Congress to end the trade embargo (AFP, 2015).
[9] The group comprised eight senators and 31 members of the House and included from the Republican side, for example, Senator Jeff Flake (R-AZ) and Representative Mark Sanford (R-SC) (AP, 2016).
[10] The fact that the Cuban president had agreed (albeit only last minute upon seeing Obama) to hold a press conference and take questions also from U.S. journalists was expressly highlighted by Deputy National Security Advisor Rhodes in a press briefing later that day as being "part

of opening up space" since it represented "an unusual occurrence" for the Cuban leader (White House, 2016d).

11. Obama stated later that "one of the individuals who was there still had cuts in his wrists from handcuffs because he had been detained just the day before" (Obama, 2016f), which in turn shows that the Cuban government engaged in coercive measures against Cuban dissidents even during Obama's visit—something that the administration was well aware of (White House, 2016d).

12. Obama also: did some family sightseeing, including Havana Cathedral; laid a wreath at the José Marti Memorial; attended a state dinner in the Palace of the Revolution; and watched a baseball game between the Tampa Bay Rays, a professional team from the United States, and the Cuban national team.

13. The Cuban reaction was more muted, though, with, for example, the president of Cuba's National Assembly, Ricardo Alcaron, dismissing Obama's reforms as "minor changes" (Lacey, 2009).

14. Obama later expressly acknowledged the role of both sides for his reengagement with Cuba. On the occasion of the pope's visit to the White House in September 2015, he stated: "Holy Father, we are grateful for your invaluable support of our new beginning with the Cuban people—which holds out the promise of better relations between our countries, greater cooperation across our hemisphere, and a better life for the Cuban people" (Obama, 2015d). In turn, in his address to the Canadian parliament in June 2016, Obama said: "I thank Canada for its indispensable role in hosting our negotiations with the Cuban government, and supporting our efforts to set aside half a century of failed policies to begin a new chapter with the Cuban people" (Obama, 2016g).

15. The administration also ended the "Cuban Medical Professional Parole Program" which offered preferential treatment for Cuban medical personnel in terms of applying for asylum in the United States.

16. In fact, Obama himself had reconsidered his position on the embargo. During the 2008 presidential campaign, he had still argued: "I will maintain the embargo. It provides us with the leverage to present the regime with a clear choice: if you take significant steps toward democracy, beginning with the freeing of all political prisoners, we will take steps to begin normalizing relations. That's the way to bring about real change in Cuba—through strong, smart and principled diplomacy" (States News Service, 2008). It was only later that he came to the conviction that the embargo must go.

four Alternative Explanations

1. While LeoGrande (2016: 30) suggests that "U.S. officials themselves were not united around the goal of the new policy" in terms of whether it

aimed at co-existence or ultimately (still) regime change, he does not provide specifics on the actors who seemingly disagreed. What is more, the disagreement as LeoGrande describes it does not suggest that there was a major pushback against Obama's normalization policy as such but rather with respect to its ultimate goal.

[2] The 2014 poll was conducted between February and May 2014; Obama delivered his "Cuba policy détente" speech in December 2014.

[3] Hillary Rodham Clinton served as secretary of state during the first four years of the Obama administration (2009–2013), during which she supported Obama's initial steps at normalization (for example, AFP, 2009). However, she was no longer in office when the fundamental changes occurred (from 2014 onward).

five Conclusion and Outlook

[1] For a discussion of practical challenges in the implementation of policy changes across a variety of issues areas (trade, investment, and so on), see, for example, Benjamin-Alvarado (2019) and Laguardia Martinez et al (2020: Chapter 6).

[2] The goal of ushering in significant steps toward a democratic transition in Cuba after Raúl Castro's resignation similarly failed to come to fruition. On Cuban domestic politics after the resignation of Castro in 2018, see, for example, Brenner et al (2020) and Bastian et al (2023).

[3] This syndrome referred to "unexplained health incidents, sometimes referred to as 'sonic attacks', affecting U.S. diplomats" (Laguardia Martinez et al, 2020: 63).

[4] On decentering FPA scholarship from its typical Western focus, see Brummer (2021).

References

Agence France Presse [AFP] (2004) Bush Attacks Kerry on Cuba Policy, August 28.

Agence France Presse [AFP] (2008) Obama's Cuba Policy Could Woo Key Exile Voters, February 26.

Agence France Presse [AFP] (2009) Obama Team Hopes Cuba Seizes Chance to Change, January 13.

Agence France Presse [AFP] (2013a) Obama-Castro Handshake a Hopeful Gesture: Cuba Gov't Website, December 10.

Agence France Presse [AFP] (2013b) Republicans Thumb Obama for Castro Handshake, December 10.

Agence France Presse [AFP] (2015) Obama Meets Raul Castro in New York, September 29.

Allison, G.T. (1971) *Essence of Decision: Explaining the Cuban Missile Crisis*, Boston: Little, Brown and Company.

Allison, G.T. and Zelikow, P. (1999) *Essence of Decision: Explaining the Cuban Missile Crisis* (2nd edn), New York: Longman.

Anderson, J.L. (2017) Donald Trump Reverses Barack Obama's Cuba Policy, *The New Yorker*, June 16, Available from: https://www.newyorker.com/news/daily-comment/donald-trump-reverses-barack-obamas-cuba-policy (Accessed December 20, 2023).

Associated Press [AP] (2007) Obama Offer to Meet Rogue Leaders Touches Off Firestorm and Clashes with Clinton, July 24.

Associated Press [AP] (2012a) Mixed Results for Obama Openness with Foreign Foes, April 14.

Associated Press [AP] (2012b) Cuba Casts Big Shadow Over Summit of Americas, April 16.

Associated Press [AP] (2012c) Cuba Rebukes Obama Over Summit Talk Democracy, April 18.

Associated Press [AP] (2012d) Obama Argues Against Romney's "Top-down Economics," September 22.

Associated Press [AP] (2013) Cuba, US Try Talking, but Face Many Obstacles, June 21.

Associated Press [AP] (2016) The Latest: White House: Castro Wasn't Expected at Airport, March 21.

BBC (2015) What is Behind the US-Cuba Thaw?, August 14, Available from: https://www.bbc.com/news/world-latin-america-30524560 (Accessed December 5, 2023).

Baker, P. (2014) U.S. to Restore Full Relations with Cuba, Erasing a Last Trace of Cold War Hostility, *New York Times*, December 17, Available from: https://www.nytimes.com/2014/12/18/world/americas/us-cuba-relations.html (Accessed November 24, 2023).

Barrett, L. (2023) Why is Biden Pursuing a Trump-lite Approach with Cuba?, *Newsweek.com*, January 20, Available from: https://www.newsweek.com/why-biden-pursuing-trump-lite-approach-cuba-opinion-1775161 (Accessed December 22, 2023).

Bastian, H., Brenner, P., Kirk, J.M. and LeoGrande, W.M. (eds) (2023) *Contemoprary Cuba. The Post-Castro Era* (3rd edn), Lanham, MD: Rowman and Littlefield.

Baumgartner, F.R., Jones, B.D. and Mortensen, P.M. (2017) Punctuated Equilibrium Theory: Explaining Stability and Change in Public Policymaking. In C.M. Weible and P.A. Sabatier (eds) *Theories of the Policy Process* (4th edn), Boulder, CO: Westview, pp 55–101.

Benjamin-Alvarado, J.C. (2019) The Ghost of Helms-Burton: Necessary Course Corrections on the Path to Normalized U.S.–Cuban Relations. In M.J. Kelly, E. Moreno, and R.C. Witmer, II (eds) *The Cuba-U.S. Bilateral Relationship. New Pathways and Policy Choices*, New York: Oxford University Press, pp 205–23.

Blavoukos, S. and Bourantonis, D. (2012) Policy Entrepreneurs and Foreign Policy Change: The Greek–Turkish Rapprochement in the 1990s, *Government and Opposition*, 47(4): 597–617.

Blavoukos, S. and Bourantonis, D. (2014) Identifying Parameters of Foreign Policy Change: An Eclectic Approach, *Cooperation and Conflict*, 49(4): 483–500.

Bovens, M. and 't Hart, P. (2016) Revisiting the Study of Policy Failure, *Journal of European Public Policy*, 23(5): 653–66.

REFERENCES

Bovens, M., 't Hart, P. and Peters, B.G. (eds) (2001a) *Success and Failure in Public Governance. A Comparative Analysis*, Cheltenham: Edward Elgar.

Bovens, M., 't Hart, P. and Peters, B.G. (2001b) Analysing Governance Success and Failure in Six European States, in M. Bovens, P. 't Hart, and B.G. Peters (eds) *Success and Failure in Public Governance. A Comparative Analysis*, Cheltenham: Edward Elgar, pp 12–29.

Brenner, P., Kirk, J.M. and LeoGrande, W.M. (eds) (2020) *Cuba at the Crossroads*, Lanham, MD: Rowman and Littlefield.

Brummer, K. (2016) "Fiasco Prime Ministers." Beliefs and Leadership Traits as Possible Causes for Policy Fiascos, *Journal of European Public Policy*, 23(5): 702–17.

Brummer, K. (2021) Advancing Foreign Policy Analysis by Studying Leaders from the Global South, *International Affairs*, 97(2): 405–21.

Brummer, K. (2023) Leadership Trait Analysis, in P.A. Mello and F. Ostermann (eds) *The Routledge Handbook of Methods of Foreign Policy Analysis*, London: Routledge, pp 238–54.

Brummer, K. (2024) Foreign Policy Analysis and Public Policy, in J. Kaarbo and C.G. Thies (eds) *The Oxford Handbook of Foreign Policy Analysis*, Oxford: Oxford University Press.

Brummer, K. and Oppermann, K. (2021) Conclusion: Grasping Foreign Policy Change. In J.K. Joly and T. Haesebrouck (eds) *Foreign Policy Change in Europe since 1991*, Cham: Palgrave Macmillan, pp 311–31.

Brummer, K. and Oppermann, K. (2024) *Foreign Policy Analysis*, Oxford: Oxford University Press.

Brummer, K., Harnisch, S., Oppermann, K., and Panke, D. (eds) (2019) *Foreign Policy as Public Policy? Promises and Pitfalls*, Manchester: Manchester University Press.

Cairney, P. (2018) Three Habits of Successful Policy Entrepreneurs, *Policy & Politics*, 46(2): 199–215.

Calmes, J. and Neuman, W. (2012) Americas Meetings Ends with Discord Over Cuba, *New York Times*, April 16, Section A, p 6.

Capano, G. and Galanti, M.T. (2018) Policy Dynamics and Types of Agency: From Individual to Collective Patterns of Action, *European Policy Analysis*, 4(1): 23–47.

Carlsnaes, W. (1992) The Agency-Structure Problem in Foreign Policy Analysis, *International Studies Quarterly* 36(3): 245–70.

Carlsnaes, W. (1993) On Analyzing the Dynamics of Foreign Policy Change: A Critique and Reconceptualization, *Cooperation and Conflict*, 28(1): 5–30.

Carter, R.G. and Scott, J.M. (2009) *Choosing to Lead. Understanding Congressional Foreign Policy Entrepreneurs*, Durham, NC: Duke University Press.

Castro Mariño, S.M. and Pruessen, R.W. (eds) (2012) *Fifty Years of Revolution. Perspectives on Cuba, the United States, and the World*, Gainesville, FL: University Press of Florida.

Charillon, F. (2018) Public Policy and Foreign Policy Analysis, in C.G. Thies (ed.) *Oxford Encyclopedia of Foreign Policy Analysis, Volume 2*, Oxford: Oxford University Press, pp 483–96.

CNN (2009) Poll: Three-Quarters Favor Relations with Cuba, April 10, Available from: http://edition.cnn.com/2009/POLITICS/04/10/poll.cuba/ (Accessed November 24, 2023).

CNN (2015) Obama & Putin Clash at United Nations; Obama & Castro to Discuss Cuba Trade Embargo; Trump Unveils Tax Proposal. Aired 4-4:30a ET. CNN Early Start, September 29. Transcript available at Lexis Nexis.

Collier, D. and Mahoney, J (1996) Insights and Pitfalls. Selection Bias in Qualitative Research, *World Politics*, 49(1): 56–91.

Congressional Research Service [CRS] (2022) Biden Administration's Cuba Policy Changes, August 11, Available from: https://crsreports.congress.gov/product/pdf/IN/IN11937/4 (Accessed December 22, 2023).

Conley, R.F. (2019) "I Too Am a Human": The Political Psychology of Pakistan's Former President General Pervez Musharraf, *South Asian Survey*, 26(2): 93–116.

Crahan, M.E. and Castro Mariño, S.M. (eds) (2016) *Cuba-US Relations: Normalization and Its Challenges*, New York: Institute of Latin American Studies.

REFERENCES

Croco, S.E. (2011) The Decider's Dilemma: Leader Culpability, War Outcomes, and Domestic Punishment, *American Political Science Review*, 105(3): 457–77.

Cruz, T. (2016) In Cuba, Obama Will Legitimize the Corrupt and Ignore the Oppressed. What's American About That?, *Politico*, March 20, Available from: https://www.politico.com/magazine/story/2016/03/obama-cuba-visit-ted-cruz-213749/ (Accessed December 13, 2023).

Cuhadar, E., Kaarbo, J., Kesgin, B., and Ozkececi-Taner, B. (2017) Personality or Role? Comparisons of Turkish Leaders across Different Institutional Positions, *Political Psychology*, 38(1): 39–54.

David, C.-P. (2015) Policy Entrepreneurs and the Reorientation of National Security Policy under the G. W. Bush Administration (2001–04), *Politics & Policy*, 43(1): 163–95.

DeYoung, K. (2016) How Obama's Trip to Havana Finally Ended the Cold War, *Washington Post*, November 18, Available from: https://www.washingtonpost.com/graphics/national/obama-legacy/us-cuba-diplomatic-relations.html (Accessed December 13, 2023).

Diamond, J. (2016) Trump Shifts on Cuba, Says He Would Reverse Obama's Deal, *CNN*, September 16, Available from: https://edition.cnn.com/2016/09/16/politics/donald-trump-cuba/index.html (Accessed December 20, 2023).

Doeser, F. (2011) Domestic Politics and Foreign Policy Change in Small States: The Fall of the Danish "Footnote Policy," *Cooperation and Conflict*, 46(2): 222–41.

Dunlop, C.A., James, S. and Radaelli, C.M. (2020) Can't Get no Learning: The Brexit Fiasco through the Lens of Policy Learning, *Journal of European Public Policy*, 27(5): 703–22.

Dyson, S.B. (2006) Personality and Foreign Policy: Tony Blair's Iraq Decisions, *Foreign Policy Analysis*, 2(3): 289–306.

Dyson, S.B. (2007) Alliances, Domestic Politics, and Leader Psychology: Why Did Britain Stay Out of Vietnam and Go into Iraq?, *Political Psychology*, 28(6): 647–66.

Dyson, S.B. (2018) Gordon Brown, Alistair Darling, and the Great Financial Crisis: Leadership Traits and Policy Responses, *British Politics*, 13(2): 121–45.

Dyson, S.B. and Raleigh, A. (2014) Public and Private Beliefs of Political Leaders: Saddam Hussein in front of a Crowd and Behind Closed Doors, *Research and Politics*, 1: 1–7.

Dyson, S.B. and Parent, M.J. (2018) The Operational Code Approach to Profiling Political Leaders: Understanding Vladimir Putin, *Intelligence and National Security*, 33(1): 84–100.

Faling, M., Biesbroek, R., Karlsson-Vinkhuyzen, S., and Termeer, K. (2019) Policy Entrepreneurship across Boundaries: A Systematic Literature Review, *Journal of Public Policy* 39(2): 393–422.

Feng, H. (2006) Crisis Deferred: An Operational Code Analysis of Chinese Leaders across the Strait, in M. Schafer and S.G. Walker (eds) *Beliefs and Leadership in World Politics. Methods and Applications of Operational Code Analysis*, Basingstoke: Palgrave Macmillan, pp 151–70.

Florida International University [FIU] (2008) 2008 Cuba/US Transition Poll. Institute for Public Opinion Research, Florida International University and The Brookings Institution. Cuba Study Group, Available from: https://cri.fiu.edu/research/cuba-poll/2008-cuba-poll.pdf (Accessed November 14, 2023).

Florida International University [FIU] (2011) 2011 Cuba Poll, Available from: https://cri.fiu.edu/research/cuba-poll/2011-cuba-poll.pdf (Accessed November 24, 2023).

Florida International University [FIU] (2014) 2014 FUI Cuba Poll. How Cuban Americans in Miami View U.S. Policies toward Cuba, Available from: https://cri.fiu.edu/research/cuba-poll/2014-fiu-cuba-poll.pdf (Accessed November, 24 2023).

Florida International University [FIU] (2016) 2016 FIU Cuba Poll. How Cuban Americans in Miami View U.S. Policies toward Cuba, Available from: https://cri.fiu.edu/research/cuba-poll/2016-cuba-poll.pdf (Accessed November 16, 2023).

Florida International University [FIU] (2018) 2018 FIU Cuba Poll. How Cuban Americans in Miami View U.S. Policies toward Cuba, Available from: https://cri.fiu.edu/research/cuba-poll/2018-fiu-cuba-poll.pdf (Accessed November 16, 2023).

REFERENCES

Fouquet, S. and Brummer, K. (2023) Profiling the Personality of Populist Foreign Policy Makers: A Leadership Trait Analysis, *Journal of International Relations and Development* 26(1): 1–29.

Frisch Aviram, N., Cohen, N., and Beeri, I. (2020) Wind(ow) of Change: A Systematic Review of Policy Entrepreneurship Characteristics and Strategies, *Policy Studies Journal*, 48(3): 612–44.

Gallup (n.d.) Cuba, Available from: https://news.gallup.com/poll/1630/cuba.aspx (Accessed November 15, 2023).

George, A.L. (1969) The "Operational Code": A Neglected Approach to the Study of Political Leaders and Decision-Making, *International Studies Quarterly*, 13(2): 190–222.

George, A.L. and Bennett, A. (2005) *Case Studies and Theory Development in the Social Sciences*, Cambridge, MA: MIT Press.

Gibbs, J.F. (2011) *US Policy Towards Cuba. Since the Cold War*, London: Routledge.

Giuliano, M. (1998) The United States' Embargo and Cuba's Foreign Relations: Missed Opportunities for Democratization, *Democratization*, 5(3): 181–99.

Gladstone, R. (2017) Trump Administration Defends Cuba Embargo at U.N., Reversing Obama, *New York Times*, November 1, Available from: https://www.nytimes.com/2017/11/01/world/americas/cuba-un-us-embargo.html (Accessed December 20, 2023).

Glueck, K. (2020) In Florida, Biden Says "I Wasn't Surprised" by Trump's Diagnosis, *New York Times*, October 5, Available from: https://www.nytimes.com/2020/10/05/us/politics/biden-florida-covid.html (Accessed December 22, 2023).

Goddard, S.E. (2009) Brokering Change: Networks and Entrepreneurs in International Politics, *International Theory*, 1(2): 249–81.

Goertz, G. and Mahoney, J. (2012) *A Tale of Two Cultures. Qualitative and Quantitative Research in the Social Sciences*, Princeton, NJ: Princeton University Press.

Goldmann, K. (1982) Change and Stability in Foreign Policy: Détente as a Problem of Stabilization, *World Politics*, 34(2): 230–66.

Gray, P. and 't Hart, P. (eds) (1998) *Public Policy Disasters in Western Europe*, London: Routledge.

Guardian (2014) Raúl Castro Hails Improved US-Cuba Relations But Calls for Embargo to Be Lifted, December 17, Available from: https://www.theguardian.com/world/2014/dec/17/raul-castro-hails-cuba-us-relations (Accessed November 16, 2023).

Gustavsson, J. (1999) How Should We Study Foreign Policy Change?, *Cooperation and Conflict*, 34(1): 73–95.

Haacke, J. (2021) Foreign Policy Entrepreneurs, Policy Windows, and "Pragmatic Engagement": Reconsidering Insights of the Multiple Streams Framework and the Obama Administration's 2009 Policy Shift Toward Military-Run Myanmar, *Foreign Policy Analysis*, 17(3): orab017.

Halperin, M.H. (1974) *Bureaucratic Politics and Foreign Policy*, Washington, DC: Brookings.

Haney, P.J. (2018) Congress and the Politics of the End of the Cuba Embargo, in J.A. Thurber, C.C. Campbell, and D.A. Dulio (eds) *Congress and Diaspora Politics. The Influence of Ethnic and Foreign Lobbying*, Albany, NY: SUNY Press, pp 167–83.

Haney, P.J. and Vanderbush, W. (1999) The Role of Ethnic Interest Groups in U.S. Foreign Policy: The Case of the Cuban American National Foundation, *International Studies Quarterly*, 43(2): 341–61.

Haney, P.J. and Vanderbush, W. (2005) *The Cuban Embargo. The Domestic Politics of an American Foreign Policy*, Pittsburgh, PA: University of Pittsburgh Press.

Harris, G. (2015) Obama and Castro Meet a Second Time as Nations Grow Closer, *New York Times*, September 30, Section A, p 6.

He, K. and Feng, H. (2013) Xi Jinping's Operational Code Beliefs and China's Foreign Policy, *Chinese Journal of International Politics*, 6(3): 209–31.

He, K. and Feng, H. (2015) Transcending Rationalism and Constructivism: Chinese Leaders' Operational Codes, Socialization Processes, and Multilateralism after the Cold War, *European Political Science Review*, 7(3): 401–26.

Healy, P. and Zeleny, J. (2007) Novel Debate Format, but the Same Old Candidates – Correction Appended, *New York Times*, July 24, Section A, p 18.

REFERENCES

Healy, P. and Zeleny, J. (2008) Debate Takes on Contentious Air for Democrats, *New York Times*, February 22, Section A, p 1.

Hermann, C.F. (1990) Changing Course: When Governments Choose to Redirect Foreign Policy, *International Studies Quarterly*, 34(1): 3–21.

Hermann, C.F. (ed.) (2012a) *When Things Go Wrong. Foreign Policy Decision Making under Adverse Feedback*, New York: Routledge.

Hermann, C.F. (2012b) What We Do When Things Go Wrong, in C.F. Hermann (ed.) *When Things Go Wrong. Foreign Policy Decision Making under Adverse Feedback*, New York: Routledge, pp 1–10.

Hermann, M.G. (1980a) Explaining Foreign Policy Behavior Using the Personal Characteristics of Political Leaders, *International Studies Quarterly*, 24(1): 7–46.

Hermann, M.G. (1980b) Assessing the Personalities of Soviet Politburo Members, *Personality and Social Psychology Bulletin*, 6: 332–52.

Hermann, M.G. (1984) Personality and Foreign Policy Decision Making: A Study of 53 Heads of Government, in D.A. Sylvan and S. Chan (eds) *Foreign Policy Decision Making. Perception, Cognition, and Artificial Intelligence*, New York: Praeger, pp 53–80.

Hermann, M.G. (2005a) Assessing Leadership Style: Trait Analysis, in J.M. Post (ed.) *The Psychological Assessment of Political Leaders. With Profiles of Saddam Hussein and Bill Clinton*, Ann Arbor, MI: University of Michigan Press, pp 178–212.

Hermann, M.G. (2005b) William Jefferson Clinton's Leadership Style, in J.M. Post (ed.) *The Psychological Assessment of Political Leaders. With Profiles of Saddam Hussein and Bill Clinton*, Ann Arbor, MI: University of Michigan Press, pp 313–323.

Hermann, M.G. (2005c) Saddam Hussein's Leadership Style, in J.M. Post (ed.) *The Psychological Assessment of Political Leaders. With Profiles of Saddam Hussein and Bill Clinton*, Ann Arbor, MI: University of Michigan Press, pp 375–386.

Hermann, M.G. (2008) Content Analysis, in A. Klotz and D. Prakash (eds) *Qualitative Methods in International Relations*, London: Palgrave Macmillan, pp 151–67.

Hermann, M.G., Preston, T., Korany, B., and Shaw, T.M. (2001) Who Leads Matters: The Effects of Powerful Individuals, *International Studies Review*, 3(2): 83–131.

Hirschfeld Davis, J. (2015a) Obama Takes His Hopes for Cuba to Summit Meeting, *New York Times*, April 9, Section A, p 12.

Hirschfeld Davis, J. (2015b) U.S. Relaxes the Rules on Dealings with Cuba, *New York Times*, September 19, Section A, p 9.

Hirschfeld Davis, J. (2015c) Year After Cuba-U.S. Thaw, Obama Says Change Will Take Time, *New York Times*, December 17, Section A, p 6.

Hirschfeld Davis, J. (2016a) With Cuba Visit, Obama Gambles on Engagement, *New York Times*, February 19, Section A, p 14.

Hirschfeld Davis, J. (2016b) Amid Thaw, Obama Picks Top Envoy to Cuba, *New York Times*, September 28, Section A, p 6.

Hirschfeld Davis, J. (2016c) Obama Moves to Further Ease Cuba Embargo, *New York Times*, October 15, Section A, p 1.

Hirschfeld Davis, J. and Archibold, R.C. (2015a) Handshake for Obama and President of Cuba, *New York Times*, April 11, Section A, p 5.

Hirschfeld Davis, J. and Archibold, R.C. (2015b) Obama Meets Cuban Leader, Making History, *New York Times*, April 11, Section A, p 1.

Hirschfeld Davis, J. and Cave, D. (2016) Cuba Meeting between Obama and Castro Exposes Old Grievances, *New York Times*, March 21, Available from: https://www.nytimes.com/2016/03/22/world/americas/obama-and-raul-castro-to-meet-in-pivotal-moment-for-us-cuba-thaw.html (Accessed December 4, 2023).

Hirschfeld Davis, J. and Robles, F. (2017) U.S. Ends Special Treatment for Cuban Migrants, *New York Times*, January 13, Section A, p 1.

Hoffmann, B. (2015) *Kuba-USA: Wandel durch Annäherung*. Hamburg: GIGA.

Holsti, K.J. (1982) *Why Nations Realign: Foreign Policy Restructuring in the Postwar World*, London: George Allen & Unwin.

Holsti, O.R. (1976) Foreign Policy Formation Viewed Cognitively, in R. Axelrod (ed.) *Structure of Decision. The Cognitive Maps of Political Elites*, Princeton, NJ: Princeton University Press, pp 18–54.

REFERENCES

Howlett, M. (2012) The Lessons of Failure: Learning and Blame Avoidance in Public Policymaking, *International Political Science Review*, 33(5): 539–55.

Janis, I.L. (1982) *Groupthink. Psychological Studies of Policy Decisions and Fiascoes* (2nd edn), Boston, MA: Houghton Mifflin.

Jennings, W., Lodge, M., and Ryan, M. (2018) Comparing Blunders in Government, *European Journal of Political Research*, 57(1): 238–58.

Joly, J.K. and Haesebrouck, T. (eds) (2021) *Foreign Policy Change in Europe since 1991*, Cham: Palgrave Macmillan.

Kaarbo, J. (2019a) A Foreign Policy Analysis Perspective on *After Victory*, *British Journal of Politics and International Relations*, 21(1): 29–39.

Kaarbo, Juliet (2019b) Conclusion: The Promise and Pitfalls of Studying Foreign Policy as Public Policy, in K. Brummer, S. Harnisch, K. Oppermann, and D. Panke (eds) *Foreign Policy as Public Policy? Promises and Pitfalls*, Manchester: Manchester University Press, pp 218–31.

Kaarbo, J. and Thies, C.G. (eds) (2024) *The Oxford Handbook of Foreign Policy Analysis*, Oxford: Oxford University Press.

Kaplowitz, D.R. (1998) *Anatomy of a Failed Embargo. U.S. Sanctions against Cuba*, Boulder, CO: Lynne Rienner.

Keller, J.W. (2005) Constraint Respecters, Constraint Challengers, and Crisis Decision Making in Democracies: A Case Study Analysis of Kennedy versus Reagan, *Political Psychology*, 26(6): 835–67.

Keller, J.W. and Foster, D.M. (2012) Presidential Leadership Style and the Political Use of Force, *Political Psychology*, 33(5): 581–98.

Keller, J.W., Grant, K.A., and Foster, D.M. (2020) Presidential Risk Propensity and Intervention in Interstate Conflicts, *Foreign Policy Analysis*, 16(3): 272–91.

Kerry, J. (2018) *Every Day is Extra*. New York: Simon and Schuster.

Kesgin, B. (2013) Leadership Traits of Turkey's Islamist and Secular Prime Ministers, *Turkish Studies*, 14(1): 136–57.

Kesgin, B. (2020) Turkey's Erdoğan: Leadership Style and Foreign Policy Audiences, *Turkish Studies*, 21(1): 56–81.

King, P.J. and Roberts, N.C. (1992) An Investigation into the Personality Profile of Policy Entrepreneurs, *Public Productivity & Management Review*, 16(2): 173–90.

Kingdon, J.W. (2011) *Agendas, Alternatives, and Public Policies* (updated 2nd edn), Boston, MA: Longman.

Kleistra, Y. and Mayer, I. (2001) Stability and Flux in Foreign Affairs: Modelling Policy and Organizational Change, *Cooperation and Conflict*, 36(4): 381–414.

Kornbluh, P. and LeoGrande, W.M. (2019) Opening Cuba— Negotiating History, in M.J. Kelly, E. Moreno and R.C. Witmer, II (eds) *The Cuba-U.S. Bilateral Relationship. New Pathways and Policy Choices*, New York: Oxford University Press, pp 17–32.

Krauthammer, C. (1990/1991) The Unipolar Moment, *Foreign Affairs*, 70(1): 23–33.

Kruck, A., Oppermann, K., and Spencer, A. (eds) (2018) *Political Mistakes and Policy Failures in International Relations*, Basingstoke: Palgrave Macmillan.

Lacey, M. (2009) In Cuba, Hopeful Tenor toward Obama is Ebbing, *New York Times*, December 31, Section A, p 6.

Laguardia Martinez, J., Chami, G., Montoute, A., and Mohammed, D.A. (2020) *Changing Cuba-U.S. Relations. Implications for CARICOM States*, Cham: Palgrave Macmillan.

Lantis, J.S. (2019) *Foreign Policy Advocacy and Entrepreneurship. How a New Generation in Congress is Shaping U.S. Engagement with the World*, Ann Arbor, MI: University of Michigan Press.

Leiro, S. (2016) The First Scheduled Flight from the U.S. Arrives in Cuba, August 31, Available from: https://obamawhitehouse.archives.gov/blog/2016/08/31/first-scheduled-flight-us-arrives-cuba (Accessed December 5, 2023).

Leites, N. (1951) *The Operational Code of the Politburo*, New York: McGraw-Hill.

Lentner, H.H. (2006) Public Policy and Foreign Policy: Divergences, Intersections, Exchange, *Review of Policy Research*, 23(1): 169–81.

LeoGrande, W.M. (2015a) A Policy Long Past Its Expiration Date: US Economic Sanctions Against Cuba, *Social Research*, 82(4): 939–66.

REFERENCES

LeoGrande, W.M. (2015b) Normalizing US-Cuba Relations: Escaping the Shackles of the Past, *International Affairs*, 91(3): 473–88.

LeoGrande, W.M. (2016a) No Time to Lose: Navigating the Shoals of the New U.S.–Cuba Relationship, in M.E. Crahan and S.M. Castro Mariño (eds) *Cuba-US Relations: Normalization and Its Challenges*, New York: Institute of Latin American Studies, pp 17–48.

LeoGrande, W.M. (2016b) What Trump Misses About Cuba, *New York Times*, December 1, Section A, p 31.

LeoGrande, W.M. (2020) Pushing on an Open Door? Ethnic Foreign Policy Lobbies and the Cuban American Case, *Foreign Policy Analysis*, 16(3): 438–56.

LeoGrande, W.M. (2023) US-Cuban Relations. The New Cold War in the Caribbean, in H. Bastian, P. Brenner, J.M. Kirk and W.M. LeoGrande (eds) *Contemporary Cuba. The Post-Castro Era*, Lanham, MD: Rowman and Littlefield, pp 217–27.

LeoGrande, W.M. and Jiménez, M.R. (2012) U.S.–Cuban Relations: Prospects for Cooperative Coexistence, in S.M. Castro Mariño and R.W. Pruessen (eds) *Fifty Years of Revolution. Perspectives on Cuba, the United States, and the World*, Gainesville, FL: University Press of Florida, pp 359–73.

LeoGrande, W.M. and Kornbluh, P. (2014) *Back Channel to Cuba. The Hidden History of Negotiations between Washington and Havana*, Chapel Hill: University of North Carolina Press.

Luo, M. (2008) Cuba Is Topic as McCain Continues Attack on Obama, *New York Times*, May 21, Section A, p 26.

Macdonald, J.M. (2015) Eisenhower's Scientists: Policy Entrepreneurs and the Test-Ban Debate 1954–1958, *Foreign Policy Analysis*, 11(1): 1–21.

Macdonald, J. and Schneider, J. (2017) Presidential Risk Orientation and Force Employment Decisions: The Case of Unmanned Weaponry, *Journal of Conflict Resolution*, 61(3): 511–36.

Malici, A. and Malici, J. (2005) The Operational Codes of Fidel Castro and Kim Il Sung: The Last Cold Warriors?, *Political Psychology*, 26(3): 387–412.

Marsh, D. and McConnell, A. (2010) Towards a Framework for Establishing Policy Success, *Public Administration*, 88(2), 564–83.

Marsh, K. and Lantis, J.S. (2018) Are All Foreign Policy Innovators Created Equal? The New Generation of Congressional Foreign Policy Entrepreneurship, *Foreign Policy Analysis*, 14(2): 212–34.

May, P.J. (1992) Policy Learning and Failure, *Journal of Public Policy*, 12(4): 331–54.

Mazarr, M.J. (2007) The Iraq War and Agenda Setting, *Foreign Policy Analysis*, 3(1): 1–23.

McConnell, A. (2010) Policy Success, Policy Failure and Grey Areas In-Between, *Journal of Public Policy*, 30(3): 345–62.

McConnell, A. (2016) A Public Policy Approach to Understanding the Nature and Causes of Foreign Policy Failure, *Journal of European Public Policy*, 23(5): 667–84.

Meijerink, S. and Huitema, D. (2010) Policy Entrepreneurs and Change Strategies: Lessons from Sixteen Case Studies of Water Transitions around the Globe, *Ecology and Society*, 15(2): 21.

Mintrom, M. (2000) *Policy Entrepreneurs and Social Choice*, Washington, DC: Georgetown University Press.

Mintrom, M. (2020) *Policy Entrepreneurs and Dynamic Change*, Cambridge: Cambridge University Press.

Mintrom, M. and Luetjens, J. (2018) Policy Entrepreneurs and Foreign Policy Decision Making, in C.G. Thies (ed.) *The Oxford Encyclopedia of Foreign Policy Analysis*, Volume 2, Oxford: Oxford University Press, pp 394–411.

Mintrom, M. and Luetjens, J. (2019) International Policy Entrepreneurship, in D. Stone and K. Moloney (eds) *The Oxford Handbook of Global Policy and Transnational Administration*, Oxford: Oxford University Press, pp 111–28.

Mintrom, M., Maurya, D., and He, A.J. (2020) Policy Entrepreneurship in Asia: The Emerging Research Agenda, *Journal of Asian Public Policy*, 13(1): 1–17.

Mintrom, M. and Norman, P. (2009) Policy Entrepreneurship and Policy Change, *Policy Studies Journal*, 37(4): 649–67.

REFERENCES

National Public Radio [NPR] (2014) Transcript: President Obama's Full NPR Interview, December 29, Available from: https://www.npr.org/2014/12/29/372485968/transcript-president-obamas-full-npr-interview (Accessed November 29, 2023).

Navot, D. and Cohen, N. (2015) How Policy Entrepreneurs Reduce Corruption in Israel, *Governance*, 28(1): 61–76.

New York Times [NYT] (2008) About Latin America, November 28, Section A, p 42.

New York Times [NYT] (2014a) Mr. Obama's Historic Move on Cuba, December 18, Section A, p 38.

New York Times [NYT] (2014b) The Moment to Restore Ties to Cuba, October 12, Section SR, p 10.

Norman, Jim (2016) Majority of Americans View Cuba Favorably for First Time, *Gallup*, February 15, Available from: https://news.gallup.com/poll/189245/majority-americans-view-cuba-favorably-first-time.aspx (Accessed December 1, 2023).

Obama, B. (2011) Remarks by President Obama on Latin America in Santiago, Chile, March 21, Available from: https://obamawhitehouse.archives.gov/the-press-office/2011/03/21/remarks-president-obama-latin-america-santiago-chile (Accessed November 20, 2023).

Obama, B. (2014a) Barack Obama: Cuba Policy Detente Address, December 17, Available from: https://www.americanrhetoric.com/speeches/barackobama/barackobamacubapolicychanges.htm (Accessed November 15, 2023).

Obama, B. (2014b) Year End Press Conference, 19 December, Available from: https://www.americanrhetoric.com/speeches/barackobama/barackobamafinal2014presser.htm (Accessed November 24, 2023).

Obama, B. (2015a) Civil Society Forum Address. April 10, 2015, Hotel El Panama, Panama City, Panama, 10 April, Available from: https://www.americanrhetoric.com/speeches/barackobama/barackobamacivilsocietyforum.htm (Accessed November 21, 2023).

Obama, B. (2015b) Post Summit of Americas Press Conference, April 11, Available from: https://www.americanrhetoric.com/speeches/barackobama/barackobamapanamapostpresser.htm (Accessed November 21, 2023).

Obama, B. (2015c) Summit of the Americas First Plenary Session Address, April 11, Available from: https://www.americanrhetoric.com/speeches/barackobama/barackobamasummitamericasplenarysession.htm (Accessed November 21, 2023).

Obama, B. (2015d) White House Welcome Address for Pope Francis, September 23, Available from: https://www.americanrhetoric.com/speeches/barackobama/barackobamapopefranciswhitehousewelcome.htm (Accessed November 30, 2023).

Obama, B. (2016a) Weekly Address: A New Chapter with Cuba, February 20, Available from: https://www.americanrhetoric.com/speeches/barackobama/barackobamaweeklyaddresscubanewchapter.htm (Accessed December 1, 2023).

Obama, B. (2016b) Remarks by President Obama at U.S. Embassy Meet and Greet—Havana, Cuba. Melia Habana Hotel, Havana, Cuba, March 20, Available from: https://obamawhitehouse.archives.gov/the-press-office/2016/03/21/remarks-president-obama-us-embassy-meet-and-greet-havana-cuba (Accessed December 4, 2023).

Obama, B. (2016c) Address to Entrepreneurs of Cuba, Havana, Cuba, March 21, Available from: https://www.americanrhetoric.com/speeches/barackobama/barackobamacubaentrepreneurs.htm (Accessed December 4, 2023).

Obama, B. (2016d) Joint Press Conference with Raul Castro, March 21, Available from: https://www.americanrhetoric.com/speeches/barackobama/barackobamaraulcastropresser.htm (Accessed December 5, 2023).

Obama, B. (2016e) Address to the People of Cuba, March 22, Available from: https://www.americanrhetoric.com/speeches/barackobama/barackobamacubapeoplespeech.htm (Accessed November 22, 2021).

Obama, B. (2016f) Post G7 Press Conference in Japan, May 26, Available from: https://www.americanrhetoric.com/speeches/barackobama/barackobamajapanpostG7presser.htm (Accessed December, 5 2023).

Obama, B. (2016g) Address to the Parliament of Canada, June 29, Available from: https://www.americanrhetoric.com/speeches/barackobama/barackobamaparliamentofcanadaspeech.htm (Accessed December 5, 2023).

Obama, B. (2016h) Young Leaders of the Americas Initiative Address, November 20, Available from: https://www.americanrhetoric.com/speeches/barackobama/barackobamaYLAI2016.htm (Accessed December 6, 2023).

Obama, B. (2017) Final Presidential Press Conference, January 18, Available from: https://www.americanrhetoric.com/speeches/barackobama/barackobamafinalpressconference.htm (Accessed December 6, 2023).

Obama, B. (2020) *A Promised Land*, New York: Crown.

Özdamar, Ö. (2017) Leadership Analysis at a "Great Distance": Using the Operational Code Construct to Analyse Islamist Leaders, *Global Society*, 31(2): 167–98.

Özdamar, Ö. and Canbolat, S. (2018) Understanding New Middle Eastern Leadership: An Operational Code Approach, *Political Research Quarterly*, 71(1): 19–31.

Özdamar, Ö. and Ceydilek, E. (2020) European Populist Radical Right Leaders' Foreign Policy Beliefs: An Operational Code Analysis, *European Journal of International Relations*, 26(1): 137–62.

Pérez, L. (2014) Cuban Americans and US Cuba Policy, in J. DeWind and R. Segura (eds) *Diaspora Lobbies and the US Government. Convergence and Divergence in Making Foreign Policy*, New York: Social Science Research Council and New York University Press, pp 132–59.

Petridou, E. and Mintrom, M. (2021) A Research Agenda for the Study of Policy Entrepreneurs, *Policy Studies Journal*, 49(4): 943–67.

Pew Research Center (2015) Most Support Stronger U.S. Ties with Cuba, January 16, Available from: https://www.pewresearch.org/politics/2015/01/16/most-support-stronger-u-s-ties-with-cuba/ (Accessed November 30, 2023).

Phillips, K. (2015) The Cuban-American Thaw, Explained, *ABC*, November 17, Available from: https://www.abc.net.au/listen/programs/rearvision/the-cuban-thaw/6944116 (Accessed December 5, 2023).

Post, J.M. (ed.) (2005) *The Psychological Assessment of Political Leaders. With Profiles of Saddam Hussein and Bill Clinton*, Ann Arbor, MI: University of Michigan Press.

Prevost, G. (2011) The Obama Administration and Cuba: The Clinton Administration Revisited, *International Journal of Cuban Studies*, 3(4): 311–27.

Rabini, C., Brummer, K., Dimmroth, K., and Hansel, M. (2020a) Profiling Foreign Policy Leaders in Their Own Language: New Insights into the Stability and Formation of Leadership Traits, *British Journal of Politics and International Relations*, 22(2): 256–73.

Rabini, C., Dimmroth, K., Brummer, K., and Hansel, M. (2020b) *Entscheidungsträger in der deutschen Außenpolitik: Führungseigenschaften und politische Überzeugungen der Bundeskanzler und Außenminister*, Baden-Baden: Nomos.

Renshon, J. (2008) Stability and Change in Belief Systems: The Operational Code of George W. Bush, *Journal of Conflict Resolution*, 52(6): 820–49.

Renshon, J. (2009) When Public Statements Reveal Private Beliefs: Assessing Operational Codes at a Distance, *Political Psychology*, 30(4): 649–61.

Rhodes, B. (2019) *The World as it Is. A Memoir of the Obama White House*, New York: Random House.

Rieff, D. (2008) Will Little Havana Go Blue?, *New York Times*, July 13, Section MM, p 46.

Roberts, N.C. and King, P.J. (1991) Policy Entrepreneurs: Their Activity Structure and Function in the Policy Process, *Journal of Public Administration Research and Theory*, 1(2): 147–75.

Rodham Clinton, H. (2014) *Hard Choices*, London: Simon and Schuster.

Rodriguez, R. and Targ, H. (2018) Trump's Cuban Policy as a Metaphor for US Politics, *International Critical Thought*, 8(4): 596–608.

REFERENCES

Rosati, J.A. (1994) Cycles in Foreign Policy Restructuring. The Politics of Continuity and Change in U.S. Foreign Policy, in J.A. Rosati, J.D. Hagan, and M.W. Sampson III (eds) *Foreign Policy Restructuring. How Governments Respond to Global Change*, Columbia, SC: University of South Carolina Press, pp 221–61.

Rubenzer, T. (2008) Ethnic Minority Interest Group Attribute and U.S. Foreign Policy Influence: A Qualitative Comparative Analysis, *Foreign Policy Analysis*, 4(2): 169–85.

Rubenzer, T. (2011) Campaign Contributions and U.S. Foreign Policy Outcomes: An Analysis of Cuban American Interests, *American Journal of Political Science*, 55(1): 105–16.

Rubenzer, T. and Redd, S.B. (2010) Ethnic Minority Groups and U.S. Foreign Policy: Examining Congressional Decision Making and Economic Sanctions, *International Studies Quarterly*, 54(3): 755–77.

Rubio, M. (2015) Obama's Faustian Bargain with Cuba, *New York Times*, July 8, Section A, p 21.

Rutenberg, J. and Zeleny, J. (2008) Obama Seeks to Clarify his Disputed Comments on Diplomacy, *New York Times*, May 29, Section A, p 18.

Schafer, M. (2000) Issues in Assessing Psychological Characteristics at a Distance: An Introduction to the Symposium, *Political Psychology*, 21(3): 511–27.

Schafer, M. and Walker, S.G. (eds) (2006a) *Beliefs and Leadership in World Politics. Methods and Applications of Operational Code Analysis*, Basingstoke: Palgrave Macmillan.

Schafer, M. and Walker, S.G. (2006b) Operational Code Analysis at a Distance: The Verbs in Context System of Content Analysis, in M. Schafer and S.G. Walker (eds) *Beliefs and Leadership in World Politics. Methods and Applications of Operational Code Analysis*, Basingstoke: Palgrave Macmillan, pp 25–51.

Schafer, M. and Walker, S.G. (2006c) Democratic Leaders and the Democratic Peace: The Operational Codes of Tony Blair and Bill Clinton, *International Studies Quarterly*, 50(3): 561–83.

Schafer, M. and Walker, S.G. (eds) (2021) *Operational Code Analysis and Foreign Policy Roles. Crossing Simon's Bridge*, London: Routledge.

Schafer, M. and Walker, S.G. (2023) Operational Code Analysis, in P.A. Mello and F. Ostermann (eds) *The Routledge Handbook of Methods of Foreign Policy Analysis*, London: Routledge, pp 255–68.

Schneider, M. and Teske, P. (1992) Toward a Theory of the Political Entrepreneur: Evidence from Local Government, *American Political Science Review*, 86(3): 737–47.

Schoultz, L. (2009) *That Infernal Little Cuban Republic. The United States and the Cuban Revolution*, Chapel Hill, NC: University of North Carolina Press.

Schwab, P. (1999) *Cuba. Confronting the U.S. Embargo*, New York: St. Martin's Press.

Seelye, K.Q. and Falcone, M. (2007) Obama Says Clinton Is "Bush-Cheney Lite," *New York Times*, July 27, Section A, p 19.

Sengupta, S. and Gladstone, R. (2016) U.S. Abstains in U.N. Vote on Embargo against Cuba, *New York Times*, October 27, Section A, p 8.

Sesin, C. (2020) Biden Slams Trump on "Abject Failure" on Venezuela, as well as Cuba Policies, *NBC News*, September 6, Available from: https://www.nbcnews.com/news/latino/biden-slams-trump-abject-failure-venezuela-well-cuba-policies-n1239356 (Accessed December 22, 2023).

Shear, M.D. (2013) Obama Reaches Out to Cuba's Leader, but the Meaning May Elude Grasp, *New York Times*, December 11, Section A, p 6.

Smith, S. (2016) 5 Facts about U.S. Relations with Cuba, *Pew Research Center*, March 18, Available from: https://www.pewresearch.org/short-reads/2016/03/18/5-facts-about-u-s-relations-with-cuba/ (Accessed December 4, 2023).

Sprout, H. and Sprout, M. (1957) Environmental Factors in the Study of International Politics, *Journal of Conflict Resolution*, 1(4): 309–28.

States News Service (23.5.2008) Remarks of Senator Barack Obama: Renewing U.S. Leadership in Americas, May 23.

Stolberg, S.G. (2008) Bush Criticizes Democrats Running for President on Trade, Iraq and Cuba, But Not by Name, *New York Times*, February 29, Section A, p 19.

REFERENCES

Stolberg, S.G. and Cave, D. (2009) Obama Opens Door to Cuba, But Only a Crack, *New York Times*, April 14, Available from: https://www.nytimes.com/2009/04/14/world/americas/14cuba.html (Accessed November 22, 2023).

Sullivan, M.P. (2022) Cuba: U.S. Restrictions on Travel and Remittances. Updated December 15, 2022, *Congressional Research Service*, Available from: https://sgp.fas.org/crs/row/RL31139.pdf (Accessed November 20, 2023).

Taysi, T. and Preston, T. (2001) The Personality and Leadership Style of President Khatami: Implications for the Future of Iranian Political Reform, in O. Feldman and L.O. Valenty (eds) Profiling Political Leaders. Cross-Cultural Studies of Personality and Behavior, Westport, CN: Praeger, pp 57–77.

The Economist (2008a) Time for a (Long Overdue) Change, December 30, Available from: https://www.economist.com/leaders/2008/12/30/time-for-a-long-overdue-change (Accessed November 24, 2023).

The Economist (2008b) End of the Embargo?, November 6, Available from: https://www.economist.com/the-world-in-2009/2008/11/06/end-of-the-embargo (Accessed November 24, 2023).

The Economist (2009) Resistant to Sticks and Carrots, November 19, Available from: https://www.economist.com/the-americas/2009/11/19/resistant-to-sticks-and-carrots (Accessed November 24, 2023).

The Economist (2014a) If Not Now, When?, April 5, Available from: https://www.economist.com/leaders/2014/04/05/if-not-now-when (Accessed November 24, 2023).

The Economist (2014b) At Last, a Thaw, December 17, Available from: https://www.economist.com/the-americas/2014/12/17/at-last-a-thaw (Accessed November 24, 2023).

The Economist (2015) Why the United States and Cuba are Cosying Up, May 29, Available from: https://www.economist.com/the-economist-explains/2015/05/29/why-the-united-states-and-cuba-are-cosying-up (Accessed November 30, 2023).

The Economist (2016a) Cuban Thaw: A History of US–Cuban Relations, March 18, Available from: https://www.economist.com/graphic-detail/2016/03/18/cuban-thaw-a-history-of-us-cuban-relations (Accessed December 4, 2023).

The Economist (2016b) Cubama, March 19, Available from: https://www.economist.com/leaders/2016/03/19/cubama (Accessed December 4, 2023).

The Economist (2017) An End to Wet Foot, Dry Foot, January 21, Available from: https://www.economist.com/the-americas/2017/01/21/an-end-to-wet-foot-dry-foot (Accessed December 6, 2023).

The Economist (2021) The Causes of Cuba's Uprising Lie at Home, July 15, Available from: https://www.economist.com/leaders/2021/07/15/the-causes-of-cubas-uprising-lie-at-home (Accessed December, 21 2023).

Trump, D. (2017) Policy of the United States towards Cuba, June 16, Available from: https://trumpwhitehouse.archives.gov/briefings-statements/remarks-president-trump-policy-united-states-towards-cuba/ (Accessed December 13, 2023).

Trump, D. (2019) Remarks to the Venezuelan American Community, February 18, Available from: https://trumpwhitehouse.archives.gov/briefings-statements/remarks-president-trump-venezuelan-american-community/ (Accessed December 13, 2023).

Trump, D. (2020) Remarks by President Trump Honoring Bay of Pigs Veterans, September 23, Available from: https://trumpwhitehouse.archives.gov/briefings-statements/remarks-president-trump-honoring-bay-pigs-veterans/ (Accessed December 13, 2023).

U.S. Department of State (2010) Cuba Migration Talks, June 18, Available from: https://2009-2017.state.gov/r/pa/prs/ps/2010/06/143367.htm (Accessed November 23, 2023).

U.S. Department of State (2015) Remarks at Flag Raising Ceremony, August 14, Available from: https://2009-2017.state.gov/secretary/remarks/2015/08/246121.htm (Accessed November 17, 2023).

U.S. Embassy in Cuba (2021) U.S. Announces Designation of Cuba as a State Sponsor of Terrorism, Available from: https://cu.usembassy.gov/u-s-announces-designation-of-cuba-as-a-state-sponsor-of-terrorism/ (Accessed December 20, 2023).

REFERENCES

Van Esch, F. and Swinkels, M. (2015) How Europe's Political Leaders Made Sense of the Euro Crisis: The Influence of Pressure and Personality, *West European Politics*, 38(6): 1203–25.

Walker, S.G. and Malici, A. (2011) *U.S. Presidents and Foreign Policy Mistakes*, Stanford, CA: Stanford University Press.

Walker, S.G. and Schafer, M. (2000) The Political Universe of Lyndon B. Johnson and His Advisors: Diagnostic and Strategic Propensities in Their Operational Codes, *Political Psychology*, 21(3): 529–43.

Walker, S.G. and Schafer, M. (2006) Belief Systems as Causal Mechanisms in World Politics: An Overview of Operational Code Analysis, in M. Schafer and S.G. Walker (eds) *Beliefs and Leadership in World Politics. Methods and Applications of Operational Code Analysis*, Basingstoke: Palgrave Macmillan, pp 3–22.

Walker, S.G. and Schafer, M., and Young, M.D. (1998) Systematic Procedures for Operational Code Analysis: Measuring and Modeling Jimmy Carter's Operational Code, *International Studies Quarterly*, 42(1): 175–90.

Walker, S.G. and Schafer, M., and Young, M.D. (1999) Presidential Operational Codes and Foreign Policy Conflicts in the Post-Cold War World, *Journal of Conflict Resolution*, 43(5): 610–25.

Walsh, J.I. (2006) Policy Failure and Policy Change. British Security Policy after the End of the Cold War, *Comparative Political Studies* 39(4): 490–518.

Waltz, K.N. (1959) *Man, the State and War: A Theoretical Analysis*, New York: Columbia University Press.

Weible, C.M., Ingold, K., Nohrstedt, D., Henry, A.D., and Jenkins-Smith, H.C. (2020) Sharpening Advocacy Coalitions, *Policy Studies Journal*, 48(4): 1054–81.

Welch, D.A. (2005) *Painful Choices. A Theory of Foreign Policy Change*, Princeton, NJ: Princeton University Press.

White, N.D. (2015) *The Cuban Embargo under International Law*, London: Routledge.

White House (2009a) Memorandum: Promoting Democracy and Human Rights in Cuba, April 13, Available from: https://obamawhitehouse.archives.gov/the-press-office/memorandum-promoting-democracy-and-human-rights-cuba (Accessed November 16, 2023).

White House (2009b) Remarks by the President at the Summit of the Americas Opening Ceremony, April 17, Available from: https://obamawhitehouse.archives.gov/the-press-office/remarks-president-summit-americas-opening-ceremony (Accessed November 22, 2023).

White House (2011) Reaching Out to the Cuban People, January 14, Available from: https://obamawhitehouse.archives.gov/the-press-office/2011/01/14/reaching-out-cuban-people (Accessed November 16, 2023).

White House (2013) Remarks by the President at the DSCC Fundraising Reception, November 8, Available from: https://obamawhitehouse.archives.gov/the-press-office/2013/11/08/remarks-president-dscc-fundraising-reception-0 (Accessed November 22, 2023).

White House (2015a) Remarks by the President in State of the Union Address, January 20, 2015, Available from: https://obamawhitehouse.archives.gov/the-press-office/2015/01/20/remarks-president-state-union-address-January-20-2015 (Accessed November 30, 2023).

White House (2015b) Remarks by President Obama and President Raul Castro of Cuba before Meeting, April 11, Available from: https://obamawhitehouse.archives.gov/the-press-office/2015/04/11/emarks-president-obama-and-president-raul-castro-cuba-meeting (Accessed November 15, 2023).

White House (2015c) Certification—Report to Congress with Respect to the Proposed Rescission of Cuba's Designation as a State Sponsor of Terrorism, April 14, Available from: https://obamawhitehouse.archives.gov/the-press-office/2015/04/14/certification-report-congress-respect-proposed-rescission-cubas-designat (Accessed November 30, 2023).

White House (2015d) Remarks by President Obama to the United Nations General Assembly, September 28, Available from: https://obamawhitehouse.archives.gov/the-press-office/2015/09/28/remarks-president-Obama-united-nations-general-assembly (Accessed November 30, 2023).

REFERENCES

White House (2016a) Remarks of President Barack Obama—State of the Union Address as Delivered, January 13, Available from: https://obamawhitehouse.archives.gov/the-press-office/2016/01/12/remarks-president-barack-obama-%E2%80%93-prepared-delivery-state-union-address (Accessed December 1, 2023).

White House (2016b) Press Briefing by Press Secretary Josh Earnest and Deputy National Security Advisor Ben Rhodes, 2/18/2016, February 18, Available from: https://obamawhitehouse.archives.gov/the-press-office/2016/02/18/press-briefing-press-secretary-josh-earnest-and-deputy-national-security (Accessed December 1, 2023).

White House (2016c) Fact Sheet: United States-Cuba Relationship, March 21, Available from: https://obamawhitehouse.archives.gov/the-press-office/2016/03/21/fact-sheet-united-states-cuba-relationship (Accessed November 14, 2023).

White House (2016d) Press Briefing by Senior Administration Officials – Havana, Cuba, 3/21/2015, March 22, Available from: https://obamawhitehouse.archives.gov/the-press-office/2016/03/22/press-briefing-senior-administration-officials-havana-cuba-3212016 (Accessed December 5, 2023).

White House (2016e) President Obama Announces another Key Administration Post, September 27, Available from: https://obamawhitehouse.archives.gov/the-press-office/2016/09/27/president-obama-announces-another-key-administration-post (Accessed December 5, 2023).

White House (2016f) Statement by the President on the Presidential Policy Directive on Cuba, October 14, Available from: https://obamawhitehouse.archives.gov/the-press-office/2016/10/14/statement-president-presidential-policy-directive-cuba (Accessed December 6, 2023).

White House (2016g) Presidential Policy Directive—United States-Cuba Normalization, October 14, Available from: https://obamawhitehouse.archives.gov/the-press-office/2016/10/14/presidential-policy-directive-united-states-cuba-normalization (Accessed December 6, 2023).

White House (2017a) Statement by the President on Cuban Immigration Policy, January 12, Available from: https://obamawhitehouse.archives.gov/the-press-office/2017/01/12/statement-president-cuban-immigration-policy (Accessed December 6, 2023).

White House (2017b) Background Briefing on the President's Cuba Policy, June 15, Available from: https://trumpwhitehouse.archives.gov/briefings-statements/background-briefing-presidents-cuba-policy/ (Accessed December 20, 2023).

White House (2017c) Fact Sheet on Cuba Policy, June 16, Available from: https://trumpwhitehouse.archives.gov/articles/fact-sheet-cuba-policy/ (Accessed December 20,2023).

White House (2018) Remarks by Vice President Pence at First Plenary Session of the Summit of the Americas, April 15, Available from: https://uy.usembassy.gov/remarks-by-vice-president-pence-at-first-plenary-session-of-the-summit-of-the-americas/ (Accessed December 21, 2023).

White House (2019) President Donald J. Trump is Taking a Stand for Democracy and Human Rights in the Western Hemisphere, April 17, Available from: https://trumpwhitehouse.archives.gov/briefings-statements/president-donald-j-trump-taking-stand-democracy-human-rights-western-hemisphere/ (Accessed December 20, 2023).

White House (2020) Remarks by President Trump in State of the Union Address, February 4, Available from: https://trumpwhitehouse.archives.gov/briefings-statements/remarks-president-trump-state-union-address-3/ (Accessed December 20, 2023).

White House (2021a) Fact Sheet: Biden-Harris Administration Measures on Cuba, July 22, Available from: https://www.whitehouse.gov/briefing-room/statements-releases/2021/07/22/fact-sheet-biden-harris-administration-measures-on-cuba/ (Accessed December 22, 2023).

White House (2021b) Remarks by President Biden at Meeting with Cuban American Leaders, July 30, Available from: https://www.whitehouse.gov/briefing-room/speeches-remarks/2021/07/30/remarks-by-president-biden-at-meeting-with-cuban-american-leaders/ (Accessed December 22, 2023).

Yang, Y.E. (2010) Leaders' Conceptual Complexity and Foreign Policy Change: Comparing the Bill Clinton and George W. Bush Foreign Policies toward China, *Chinese Journal of International Politics*, 3(4): 415–46.

Zeleny, J. (2008) Obama, in Miami, Calls for Engaging with Cuba, *New York Times*, May 24, Section A, p 15.

Ziv, G. (2011) Cognitive Structure and Foreign Policy Change: Israel's Decision to Talk to the PLO, *International Relations*, 25(4): 426–54.

Index

References to figures appear in *italic* type; those in **bold** type refer to tables. References to endnotes show both the page number and the note number (133n13).

A

"Address to the People of Cuba" (Obama) 61
adjustment change (Hermann) 20
advocacy coalitions 39
agency of decision makers 4
Alcaron, Ricardo 133n13
Allison, G.T. 110
alternative explanations 107–16, 119
alternative paths of action 27
analyzing speeches 74–6, *75*, 127, *127*
Anderson, J.L. 121
"Anglo-American" norming group (LTA) 80, **81**
appeasement 100
assessing policies 48–9
at-a-distance assessment techniques 41, 49, 51

B

back-channel exchanges 92
Baker, P. 102
behavioral implications of political beliefs 31, **32–3**
belief in the ability to control events (BACE) 41, **44**, 45
  Barack Obama **81**, 82
  Donald Trump **130**
Biden, Joe 125
Bilateral Commission 93
bilateral relations 59, 60, 84, 87
bipartisan pushback *see* pushback
Blavoukos, S. 27
Bourantonis, D. 27
bureaucratic advocacy (Hermann) 12
bureaucratic politics model 110
bureaucratic pressure 12, 110–12
Bush, George W.
  beliefs after 9/11 30
  changes in foreign policy 117
  Cuban policies 67, 71, 92
  OCA profiles 50–1
  operational code 73–4, 105
  political beliefs 73, 74–6, *75*
  sanctions policies 58

C

Calmes, J. 86
campaign promises 100
Canada 92, 133n14
Carter, Jimmy 58
Castro, Fidel 56, 58, 85
Castro, Raúl
  addressing UNGA 132n8
  challenges with US 132n3
  meeting Barack Obama 67, 84–8, 93, 100–1
  and normalization processes 126
  press conferences 132n10
  telephone call with Obama 62–3
Cave, D. 88, 92
change agents 3, 15–16, 46, 47, 117
Clinton, Bill 85, 95
Clinton, Hillary Rodham 14, 72, 111, 114
CNN 87
cognition and cognitive abilities 4–5, 6
Cold War 58, 109
commerce 102
commercial flights 63, 77

INDEX

computer-based quantitative content analysis 50
conceptual complexity (CC) 41, **44**, 45
  Barack Obama **81**, 82
  Donald Trump **130**
congruence tests 49
consular services 121
Coolidge, Calvin 87
cooperation and conflict themes 31
cooperative measures 58, 78, 105
core groups 39
criticisms *see* pushback
Cruz, Ted 101
Cuba
  differences with 59–60
  direct engagement with people 88
  dissidents 133n11
  engaging with leadership 67
  entrepreneurs 64, 88
  isolating 86
  reactions to reforms 133n13
  revolution 56
  youth leaders 64
Cuba beliefs 76, 77–8, 122–3
Cuban-American National Foundation 66
Cuban Americans 112–14, 115
Cuban Assets Control Regulations 58
Cuban Democracy Act 1992 58
Cuban Liberty and Democratic Solidarity Act 1996 58
Cuban Medical Professional Parole Program 133n15
"Cuban thaw" 1
"Cuba Policy Détente" Address (Obama, 2014) 54–5, 76
  announcing reforms 92–3
  and Congress 98
  coordinated announcements 62–3
  failure of U.S.–Cuba policy 68–9
  implementing 79–80
  joined interests and collaboration 60
  normalization process 95–6
  state sponsors of terrorism list 89
  support 113

D

David, C-P. 34
"deeds" *see* "words" and "deeds"
DeLaurentis, Jeffrey 90–1, 94
democracy 59, 62
Democratic party 71, 72
DeYoung, K. 1
diagnosing policy failures 65–70, 124
  see also policy failures
dictionary-based coding schemes 52
diplomatic relations 56, 58, 112
direct flights 77
distrust of others (DIS) 42, 43–4, **44**
  Barack Obama **81**, 82
  Donald Trump **130**

E

The Economist 70–1, 87, 123
Edwards, John 72
Eisenhower, Dwight D. 56
electoral considerations 77, 78–9
emphasis on rewards (I-5) 75, 75
ends-means relationships 76
engagement policies 84
entrepreneurial instruments and strategies 18–20, 43–7, **44**, 91, 106
environmental factors 17
explanatory frameworks of foreign policy 5
external shocks (Hermann) 12, 109–10

F

family-related travel 62
financial transactions 77, 102
  see also remittances
Florida 112–13, 115
follow-up polls 113, 134n2

Ford, Gerald 58
Foreign Policy Analysis (FPA) 2–3, 11–12, 17, 35–6, 118
foreign policy changes 2–9, 24, 27–8, 47–8, 117–18, 124
see also major foreign policy changes; policy failures
FPA literature 3–7, 11, 16, 24, 52–3
Francis, Pope 92, 133n14
future research 124–6

G

Global South 108
Goddard, S.E. 17–18
Gross, Alan 62
guiding change
  cooperative U.S.–Cuba policies 72–4
  foreign policies 18, 46–7
  political beliefs **19**, 26–33, 49
"guiding phases" 53
Gustavsson, J. 4, 5, 17, 131n1

H

Haacke, J. 131n4
Haney, P.J. 114
Harper, Stephen 86
Harris, G. 87
Havana syndrome 121, 134n3
Helms-Burton Act 1996 58
Hermann, C.F.
  bureaucratic advocacy 12
  leaders as change agents 3, 15–16
  leaders' cognition 5
  major foreign policy changes 59, 118
  policy failures and foreign policy changes 24
  problem/goal changes and international orientation changes 48
  typologies 20, 21–2, 55–6
Hermann, M.G. 42
hierarchical power relations 108–9
Hirschfeld Davis, J. 88, 89, 101, 103, 111

historical-oriented perspectives 10
Holsti, K.J. 3–4, 20
human rights 59, 62

I

implementing change 18, **19**, 49, 51, 61–2, 106
  see also policy entrepreneurs
implementing foreign policy changes 47
implementing phases 53
individual beliefs and expected behavior 31
in-group bias (IGB) 42, 43–4, **44**
  Barack Obama **81**, 82
  Donald Trump **130**
initiation (triggering change) 104–5
institutional environments 97
instrumental beliefs (OCA) 28–30, **29**
international orientation change (Hermann) 20, 21–2, 48, 55–6
international pressure 11–12, 108–10
International Relations (IR) literature 17
irreversible policy changes 120

J

Johannesburg, South Africa 85
Johnson, Lyndon B. 30

K

Kaarbo, J. 17
Kennedy administration 56
Kerry, John 90, 111, 132n4
Kingdon, J.W. 36
Kleistra, Y. 4
Kornbluh, P. 78, 92, 103
Krauthammer, C. 109

L

Laguardia Martinez, J. 10, 121
leader-centered theory 25, 43

INDEX

"leader-centered theory of foreign policy change" 5–6, 7–9, 118
leaders
 as change agents 3, 15–16, 46, 47, 117
 foreign policy drivers 4–5
leadership styles (Hermann) 42
Leadership Trait Analysis (LTA) 7, 16, 18, 40–3, 118
 coding schemes 80, **81**
 and FPA 35–6
 leadership traits 41–2
 "norming group" 45–6
 Barack Obama 80–2, **81**, 106
 and OCA 41, **50**, 51–2
 source text requirements **50**
 Donald Trump 123, 129, **130**
 see also policy entrepreneurs
leadership traits
 entrepreneurial instruments 43
 "high" and "low" manifestations 45
 scaling-up advocacy efforts 91
leading by example 39–40, 43, **44**, 45, 83–91, **83**
LeoGrande, W. M. 58, 70, 78, 92
 Cuban community 112
 "historic reversal" policy change 55
 Barack Obama's policy détente 114
 opening U.S. embassy 90
 pushback 103
 structural factors 107
 U.S.–Cuba policy changes 10–11, 14
Lew, Jacob 111
Luetjens, J. 34, 35, 40
Luo, M. 78

M

Maduro, Nicolás 121
major foreign policy changes 20–1, 23–4, 104
 see also foreign policy changes
major policy failures 22–6, 105
 see also policy failures
Marsh, D. 24–5

Mayer, I. 4
McCain, John 14, 71, 72, 100, 114
McConnell, A. 24–5
Menendez, Robert 101, 102, 103
Miami, Florida 68
micro-action and macro-outcomes (Goddard) 17–18
minor changes 20
Mintrom, M. 34, 35–40
multi-causal frameworks 5
Myanmar 131n4

N

National Public Radio (NPR) 77
National Security Presidential Memorandum NSPM-5 120
need for power (PWR) 41, **44**, 45
 Barack Obama **81**, 82
 Donald Trump **130**
networks 39
Neuman, W 86
New York Times (NYT) 54–5, 70
"non-case" policies 125
normalization policies 62, 76–7, 78, 84, 93–4, 95–6, 100
 see also U.S.–Cuban relations
Norman, P. 36, 37, 38–9
"norming groups" (LTA) 45–6, 52, 131n5

O

Obama, Barack
 family sightseeing 133n12
 leadership traits 80–1, **81**
 meeting Raúl Castro 67, 84–8, 93, 100–1
 operational codes 73–4, 105
 policy entrepreneur 82–91, **83**
 political beliefs on Cuba 74–8, *127*
 presidential campaign 2008 100
 second presidential term 77, 94–5
 second term 79
 speeches 74–6, *75*

Operational Code Analysis
(OCA) 7, 49–52, 118
  George W. Bush 74–6, **75**
  computer-based quantitative
  content analysis 50
  at-a-distance assessment
  techniques 41, 49
  identifying leaders' political
  beliefs 18, 28–31, **29**
  and LTA **50**, 51–2
  Barack Obama 74–6, **75**
Organization of American States
(OAS) 85–6

P

parliamentary democracies 126
Pence, Mike 123
philosophical beliefs (OCA)
28–30, **29**
policy entrepreneurial
actions 43, **44**
policy entrepreneurial
instruments 43, 91, 106
policy entrepreneurs 16, 34–40,
82–91, **83**
  see also implementing change;
  Leadership Trait Analysis (LTA)
policy failures 4, 16, 22–6
  and choice dilemmas 125–6
  diagnosing 65–70, 124
  as an opportunity 23–4
  policy entrepreneurs 37
  policy learning and policy
  change 27
  political beliefs 27
  trade embargos 70–1
  U.S.–Cuba policies 10, 65–70,
  105, 119
  see also foreign policy changes;
  major policy failures;
  triggering changes
policy instruments (I-4b) 75, *75*
policy-oriented perspectives 10
political beliefs 26–33, **32–3**,
46–7, 74–6, *75*
political considerations 25, 105–6
political environment (P-1) 31

political goals (I-1) 31
political goals with respect to Cuba
(P-2) 75
political maneuvering 38
political prisoners 132n2
political support 132n4
predictability of future
developments (P-3) 75, *75*
presidential campaign 2008 100, 114
Presidential Policy Directive
(PPD-43) 94, 96
"primary change agents"
(Hermann) 3
prisoner swaps 62
private networks 39
problem/goal change (Hermann)
20, 21–2, 48, 55–6
process dimensions 24–5
professional networks 39
Profiler Plus software 50, 51, 52,
74, 80
profiling 41, 74
program change (Hermann) 20
programmatic dimensions 24
prospect theory 5
psychological perspectives 17
public policy literature 16, 24
public policy scholarship 7–8
public support 95–6, 112, 114
Punctuated Equilibrium
Theory 21
pushback 71–2, 77, 100–4, 122
Putin, Vladimir 117

R

Reagan, Ronald 58
realist, threat-oriented
perspectives 13
remittances 61–2
  see also financial transactions
Renshon, J. 30
Republicans 71, 78, 101
resistance within government 25
rhetoric and actions *see* "words"
and "deeds"
Rhodes, Ben 92, 93, 106,
111, 132n10

risks in policies (I-3) 75, *75*
Robles, F. 103
role of chance (P-5) 75, *75*
Romney, Mitt 14, 101
Rosati, J.A. 20
Ros-Lehtinen, Ileana 100
Rubio, Marco 101–3, 123

S

sanctions policies 108–9
scaling up advocacy efforts 43, **44**, 45, 83, **83**, 91–6, 106
Schafer, M. 30
self-confidence (SC) 41, **44**, 45
  Barack Obama **81**, 82
  Donald Trump **130**
Social Science Automation 50
societal pressure 12, 112–15
speeches 74–6
spontaneous statements 80
Sprout, H. 6, 17
Sprout, M. 6, 17
State of the Union Address 2016 (Obama) 98
State of the Union Address 2020 (Trump) 122
state sponsors of terrorism list 77, 89, 121, 125
state visit (2016) 63, 77, 87–9, 93, 99, 101
Stolberg, S.G. 72, 92
"Strengthening the Policy of the United States toward Cuba" (NSPM–5) 120
structural factors 6, 107
Summit of the Americas
  5th Summit, Port-of-Spain, Trinidad and Tobago (2009) 67–8, 86
  6th Summit, Cartagena, Colombia (2012) 59, 60, 68, 86
  7th Summit, Panama City, Panama (2015) 60–1, 85–6, 93
  8th Summit, Lima, Peru (2018) 123
support for policies 25

T

task focus (TASK) 42, 43–4, **44**, 52
  Barack Obama **81**, 82
  Donald Trump **130**
team building 38–9, 43–4, **44**
theory-driven explanations 10
tight-knit teams 39
trade and travel 63
trade embargos
  and Congress 97–100, 106, 121, 132n8
  as a failure 70–1
  imposing 56
  Barack Obama changing opinion on 133n16
  public support to end 112
  and state sponsors of terrorism list 89–90
  and Donald Trump 125
  UNGA resolutions against 98–9
  workarounds 63
transforming institutions 40, 43, **44**, 45, **83**, 96–104, 106
travel restrictions 61–2, 77, 102
triggering changes 18, **19**, 38, 48–9
  see also policy failures
triggering foreign policy changes 46
"triggering phase" 53
Trump, Donald 114–15, 120–5
  LTA profile 123, **130**
  policy entrepreneur 129
  political beliefs 127–8, *127*
  U.S.–Cuba policies 120–1
two-tailed t-tests 50, *75*, *127*
typology of changes 20

U

"unipolar moment" (Krauthammer) 109
United Nations General Assembly (UNGA) 87, 98–9, 121, 125, 132n8

"United States–Cuba Normalization" (PPD-43) 94, 96
USAID 62
U.S. ambassador to Cuba 90–1, 94
U.S. Congress 62, 97–100, 103–4, 106
U.S.–Cuban relations 9–11, 56, **57**
see also normalization policies
U.S.–Cuba policies
  assessments 70–2
  changes under Barack Obama 55–6, 76–9
  core tenets 56–8
  differences with Cuban government 59–60
  isolating Cuba 86
  key changes 58–64, **64**
  policy failures 10, 65–70, 105, 119
  reforms 91–3
  reorienting 73
  Donald Trump 120–4
U.S. embassy, Havana 63, 87, 90, 91, 121
U.S. Senate 78

V

Venezuela 121
"Verbs in Context System" (VICS) 50, 74

W

Walker, S.G. 30
Walsh, J.I. 131n2
Waltz, K.N. 3
Welch, D.A. 4, 5, 24
"wet foot, dry foot" policy 95, 96, 103
White, N.D. 104
"words" and "deeds" 48, 59, 61–2, 64, **64**, 104

X

Xi Jinping 117

Y

Yang, Y.E. 5–6, 43

Z

Zelikow, P. 110
Ziv, G. 5–6